BAPTIZED
for THIS
MOMENT

BAPTIZED *for* THIS MOMENT

Rediscovering Grace
All Around Us

STEPHEN PAUL BOUMAN

BAPTIZED OR THIS MOMENT
Rediscovering Grace All Around Us
by Stephen Paul Bouman

Foreword and Points for Reflection and Discussion
by Rev. Stacy Martin, MDiv, MBA

Edited by Michael Coyne
Cover design, interior design, and typesetting by Patricia A. Lynch
Cover image under license from Bigstock

Published by In Extenso Press
Distributed exclusively by ACTA Publications, 4848 N. Clark Street,
Chicago, IL 60640, (800) 397-2282, actapublications.com

Scripture quotations are from the *New Revised Standard Version Bible*, Copyright © 1989
by the Division of Christian Education of the National Council of Churches of Christ in
the USA, and are used by permission.

Quotations from Kathleen O' Connor are from "O God Pay Attention: The Book of
Lamentations and the Cry to be Heard," a lecture on Lamentations given at Boston
College, The Beck Lectures #1, Boston, October 21-23, 2001.

Library of Congress Catalog Number: 2016955964
ISBN: 978-0-87946-983-2
Printed in the United States of America by Total Printing Systems
Year 25 24 23 22 21 20 19 18 17 16
Printing 15 14 13 12 11 10 9 8 7 6 5 4 3 2 First

♻ Text printed on 30% post-consumer recycled paper

To my mother of sainted memory, Victoria,
who taught me to see and express grace in the world.

To my father, Paul, still making beautiful music,
who taught me to hear grace all around us.

To my wife, Janet,
who continues to grace my life.

CONTENTS

Foreword / 9
An Incarnational Lens
by Stacy Martin

Chapter One / 13
Grace

Chapter Two / 25
From Lamentations to Anger to Comfort and Renewal

Chapter Three / 41
Public Crises, Public Re-enchantment

Chapter Four / 55
Public Church for the Life of the World

Chapter Five / 75
From Private Liturgy to Public Mission

Chapter Six / 89
The Public Mission Table

Chapter Seven / 113
Congregations and Community Organizing

Chapter Eight / 129
Interfaith Dialogue, Race, and Immigration:
New Tables Beyond Anger

Chapter Nine / 151
Resurrection

Acknowledgments / 165

About the Author / 167

CONTENTS

Foreword

About the Author / 167

AN INCARNATIONAL LENS

"Don't open that," I heard my eldest daughter's whispered warning in another room.

"Why not?" her little sister pled.

"That," came the stern reply, "is where Mom keeps her God clothes."

The "God clothes" appear on occasions that are as imaginative and mysterious as any tales spun by C.S. Lewis himself. They're worn while serving bread and wine at a table where Christ is both host and guest, while welcoming children into the ancient covenant of Beloved Community, while celebrating the unity of two lives knit together in solidarity and equality, while acknowledging the saintly and sinner within each of us during Sunday morning confession, and while honoring the blessedness of life at the grave. These occasions are at once mystical and mundane, sacred and scary. Above all, perhaps, enchanted. Imbued with power and meaning through our connection with our own improbable history.

I had been ordained a good ten years before considering in earnest the logic behind clergy vestments. And, to be honest, I wouldn't have considered them with any degree of seriousness had it not been for my daughters. Children's innocent fascination leads to questions. Lots of them. The best question one of them offered during their God clothes fascination phase was in response to the cursory answer I gave to one of their many, "Why?" questions. I'd offered—for the hundredth time and in a bit of exasperation—that pastors wear collars and funny robes to be a symbol of God's love in the world. I explained that it is easy for people to see and understand a clergy collar or a cassock as representing the unfolding presence of God's love in the world. My youngest daughter, our most prying, begged the question and rejoined, "That doesn't make sense. Shouldn't it be the other way around?"

"How do you mean?" I asked, all of a sudden genuinely interested in the conversation.

"Well, shouldn't they bring the world into church?" She remarked in an imperative tone.

Her question gave me pause. It's a question I've wrestled with ever since, and it's the question that lies at the heart of what Bishop Stephen Bouman invites us to consider in *Baptized for this Moment: Rediscovering Grace All Around Us*.

The incarnation is Christianity's great gift to the world's faith traditions. It opens our collective imagination when we read of the boundlessness of God's love through an incarnational lens. That we were invited, as humans, to care for God-in-flesh as infant and to accompany God-in-flesh as outcast—all the way to execution—is also the great paradox of our Christian faith. Typically, we tend to confuse the role of divine caregiver with the divine itself. In other words, we often assume our role as the faithful to be that of wearing God, or at least God's love, into the world, whether we are adorned with the proper trappings or not.

I tried to be careful in teaching my daughters not to conflate the church building with God's dwelling, repeating this call-and-response on Sundays:

Call: "Where does God live?"
Response: "Everywhere!"
Call: "Is church God's house?"
Response: "No. God lives everywhere!"

We do, indeed, find grace, all around us, if only we are willing to see it. But my explanation about "God clothes" trounced all previous attempts at proper theological pedagogy. In explaining that special clothes are needed to express God's love in the world, I had cast God squarely within the confines of someplace other than the everywhere of the whole wide world, namely the church building. That, just as the "God clothes" themselves cloister in a closet, we may errantly cloister our living God within church buildings, to be paraded around on Sundays and special occasions, as long as the right costume is worn by God's legitimized representatives.

It's not that we really believe that God resides in church buildings. We know better. But our actions often imply that the world has no place in church. The world is too messy and an hour on Sunday doesn't leave us enough time to clean things up. This might not be a problem were it not for the theological conundrum of Christ's incarnation. As Bishop Bouman outlines in the pages that follow, we've spent so much time trying to figure out how to get the church out into the world, we've forgotten to invite the world in to our churches.

We, as mainline Christians, find ourselves a faithful remnant of sorts at a point in history in which one might legitimately argue things have never been so good for humanity. More people have access to clean water, education, and basic needs than at any time in history. In places like China, rates of poverty have dramatically diminished in the last few generations. We still have so far to go, but, my, how far we've come. Yet on the church front, headlines about the progressive Christian landscape aren't as heartening. Every mainline denomination in the U.S. faces aging congregations, declining membership rolls, and waning financial support. It's an almost Dickensian condition, then, that we mainline Christians find ourselves in: it's at once the best of times and the worst of times.

In what follows, Bishop Bouman invites us to consider a life of faith free of cynicism. He invites us not to shelter from public calamities—terrorist attacks, natural disasters, acts of horror in our communities, insidious racism, violence on our streets, our own powerlessness in the face of both man-made and natural forces beyond our control—but to engage with others in responding to them in the light of our rich religious heritage, as a community that understands that, amidst our sorrow and anger and fear and lamentations, grace abides. He invites us to consider a faithful life as one that is measured by our willingness to question rather than by the orthodoxy of our answers. And he invites us to consider what our congregational lives might be if, instead of worrying about how to get the word out to the world, we opt to simply invite the world in.

In offering a pastoral dispatch grounded in the breadth and depth of his ministry experience, coupled with his abiding love of the Church, Bishop Bouman paints a spiritual landscape for those of us who long for renewal but require vision. It's intentionally provocative and at times disarming, a bit like moving the "God clothes" from the depths of the closet to the front room mantel. He gently reminds us that a heart unprovoked may too easily become a heart that is closed. I encourage you to explore this book and apply its insights and inquiries to your own spiritual community. May you find in its pages the profound challenge and the great comfort that comes with choosing a life of faith.

Stacy Martin, MDiv, MBA
Communications & Development Officer
Lutheran Services Florida

CHAPTER ONE

GRACE

New York: September 11, 2001

A Beautiful Fall Morning

On September 10, 2001 our daughter Rachel moved into a Manhattan apartment on 61st Street in the shadow of the Queensboro Bridge, with three guys from Dublin, a guy from Paris, and a woman from Omaha— strangers all. On the morning of September 11 she was to go to work downtown at Lutheran Social Services, around the corner from the World Trade Center.

On the morning of September 11 my wife Janet headed into New York City from our home in Rockland County, about twenty miles north of the city. She was going to a meeting, also at Lutheran Social Services downtown.

On the morning of September 11 our son Jeremy rose in Jersey City to pack for a noon flight from Kennedy Airport to Nairobi, Kenya. He was going to visit our son Timothy and daughter-in-law Erin, who were teachers in Bukoba, Tanzania, on Lake Victoria.

On the morning of September 11 Timothy and Erin woke up to teach their classes at the Kibeta English Medium School. They were anticipating Jeremy's visit, which was to include a climb up Mount Kilimanjaro.

I remember driving across the George Washington Bridge early on the morning of September 11 because the sky was so unusually blue, the air warm and clear, the view of the buildings stunning in the bright sunlight. The skyline was moored by the downtown twin towers and I smiled looking at them from the car, as I always did upon entering the city I have loved for so many years.

A few hours later I was sitting in my office on the 16th floor of the Interchurch Center at 120th Street and Riverside Drive, with windows facing south. I was meeting with two of my staff. At a little after nine I noticed black smoke rising in the distance. "Jersey," I remembered thinking and gave it no more thought. We had lived for eleven years in New Jersey and were familiar with the dirty-socks smell of the Turnpike near the airport, and of all the lousy Jersey jokes told by all the world. The smoke continued to rise in the background as we met. I was getting a little curious when my administrative assistant rushed into my office. I will never forget the stricken look on her face. "Turn on your radio. Look at the computer. There's been an attack downtown." We all bolted to the window. The towers were wreathed in smoke, black clouds hovering over the harbor, cutting through the perfect autumn blue. And so it began.

Like the rest of the world we began to seek out family. One of our staff was trying to reach a nephew who was a waiter in the towers, working a breakfast on a high floor. I could not get a call through to Lutheran Social Services but was able to reach a leader in our synod whose law office overlooks New York Harbor downtown. There was no answer at the office of Lars Qualben, a vice president for Marsh McClennan, whose office was on the ninety-second floor of Tower Two. My wife called. She was stopped at the George Washington Bridge and was able to make a U-turn and get back home. No word from Rachel or Jeremy. A second plane roared down the Hudson, past our office. Our air force scrambling, I thought, not knowing the plane was headed toward the World Trade Center. Someone watching on his computer came in and told us it had been flown into the second tower.

We watched the buildings fall, the downtown skyline obliterated in smoky ash, enveloping everything.

At noon we met to pray in the chapel of the Interchurch Center. Hundreds gathered. My part was simple. I said the Twenty-third Psalm from memory. I invited people as our prayer to name the names before God of those downtown about whom we were worried, whose fate was unknown to us. My life changed in hearing the names come at me through clenched teeth, strained voices, sobs, shouts. "Rachel, Jeremy, Lars," I muttered, adding my own names.

I called our churches in Manhattan. They were starting to receive refugees from the carnage. I encouraged and prayed with the pastors who were meeting the horror with cold water, open sanctuaries, and a simple listening embrace. The time of lamentations in New York had begun. People began calling to tell their stories of rescue, loss, worry. They gave me names to pray over. Plans for communal prayer, participation in rescue, and disaster response began to be formed.

Sometimes the phones worked, sometimes not. Cell phones were especially unreliable. Maybe that's why I haven't heard from Rachel, I prayed. At one point President David Benke of the Atlantic District of the Lutheran Church, Missouri Synod—my partner as Lutheran leader in New York and a dear friend—called. He was stuck in Brooklyn and wanted to know where I could use him. No one could get into Manhattan. I asked him to go to Lutheran Medical Center in Sunset Park, Brooklyn, designated as a primary trauma center. He stayed there into the evening, through the initial rush of wounded, then through the long waiting as only a few more came and the scale of the horror revealed itself. In mid-afternoon I spoke to Anthony Harris, the director of Lutheran Social Services. The engine of the first plane had fallen through the roof of the building of LSS on Park Row around the corner from the towers and ignited a fire. They had to evacuate everyone from the building: staff, foster children, other clients. They went north, joining the soot-covered retreat, and arrived safely at St. John's Lutheran Church at Christopher Street in Greenwich Village. I still did not know if our daughter had gone to her meeting in that building which was now burning.

Jeremy called. His trip, of course, had been canceled. It would be days before any flights entered or left the city. Jeremy and his fiancée had walked the few blocks to the river and watched the inferno from the Jersey side of the harbor. They helped those who escaped by boat and then made their way back to Jersey City.

Janet called. Rachel had slept in. She was safe. It would be another day before we could get a call through to Tanzania. Timothy told us that Bishop Buberwa and some others had come to their home and prayed with them for their beleaguered city. For days people stopped them on the streets: "*Poli sana*," they said. In Swahili: "We are so sorry."

My urge to get home was overwhelming, but I spent the rest of the afternoon and early evening on the phone, getting a sense of what was happening downtown, checking in with many people, formulating the beginning of plans that would evolve into Lutheran Disaster Response New York. As the sun descended I just wanted to hold my wife. At the entrance ramp for the George Washington Bridge I waited in a line of snarling traffic. A bomb scare had closed the bridge. I saw for the first time what would become a familiar sight: People with guns looking into cars. I drove on the shoulder, showed my clerical collar to someone with a gun, and received permission to make a U-turn back into the city. In the smoky evening I was the only car traveling south on the east side FDR expressway. I got off at 96th Street and drove through empty streets to our apartment, where we usually stayed during the week, at 88th and Lexington.

I walked out to get a slice of pizza and looked down Lexington. Downtown was shrouded in a pillar of smoke and fire of biblical proportions.

Weary people were trudging home, eyes glazed. People greeted one another in muted tones. Dazed New Yorkers began telling stories. It was somber. My collar seemed an invitation. People asked for prayer. "Father, will you pray for Vinnie? I don't think he made it." It took me an hour and a half to walk the two blocks back to our apartment.

The walls of the apartment closed in on me. After talking to each stateside member of my family, I went to the car and tried to get out again. I wanted to be with Janet. The bridge was free. I couldn't look downtown. All along the Palisades as I traveled north was the sound of sirens as fire, police, and rescue vehicles rushed south from Hudson Valley cities and towns toward Ground Zero. We were one connected village in the sprawling New York metropolis that night. Ground Zero was a hole fifty feet deep, but it was symbolically fifty miles wide. It would be Wednesday before I was able to return to the city. Shortly after I crossed the George Washington Bridge the authorities shut down all the bridges and tunnels and locked Manhattan down.

Home. Tears and embraces. Janet and I watched coverage long into the night. We called our pastor and arranged for a prayer service at our church for the next morning. We poured a drink. We prayed. We were but one family in New York near the end of a long day, repeating what millions around the world experience in natural and human-made disasters. This book is about how congregations can respond, compassionately yet effectively, to such tragic events.

Endless Day

That long day did not seem to end. In fact, the many weeks and months ahead would seem like a single endless day, as losses were accounted for, life as we knew it changed irrevocably, and certain war loomed. Endless day as we learned of the forty-seven children in our Lutheran schools who lost parents. Endless day as we lived through the memorial and burial season, remembering the dead. Endless day as terror changed the landscape of our metropolis. Endless day as the residue of trauma, depression, anger, grief, sadness, and doubt bore through the initial adrenalin rush of response and courage and deep faith, leading to spiritual enervation, despite an overweening sense of hopelessness. Endless day as the stranger among us became hunted and blamed, as the economic migrants and the poor plunged into deeper poverty in the ruined economic landscape. Endless day as initial global solidarity was lost in the run up to pending wars in Afghanistan and Iraq. How we longed for the night and true rest.

But my memories are also about spiritual rest, communal prayer, countless acts of solidarity, kindness, and compassion. Rest and refreshment came in hearing the words of the Bible as if for the first time. As we read the old, old story into our unfolding narrative, Scripture came alive.

We came at last to understand that we were baptized for this moment.

It carried us. Isaiah 62 reminded us that we would be called "a city not forgotten." In Isaiah 58 we grasped our vocation to be "healers of the breach, restorers of streets to live in." Baptism took on new meaning when we heard how one of our Lutheran chaplains, William Wrede, had run across the Brooklyn Bridge to the towers the morning of the attacks and anointed with oil the brave fire and rescue personnel who asked for this baptismal reminder as they rushed into the towers and up the smoky stairs. We came at last to understand that we were baptized for this moment. We rested in telling our stories and speaking our pain, encouraged by the opening words of Lamentations: "How lonely sits the city...." We saw the heroes in the towers as angels ascending and descending on Jacob's ladder. For a brief time our houses of worship were the most important places in the community and the Bible was a living document of drama encompassing our own.

In the weeks after 9/11, I would visit each of the eighteen conferences of our synod with only one question: How is your soul? The stories which unfolded were a part of the lamentations, which must come before the beginnings of healing. The week after September 11, President Benke and I had formed Lutheran Disaster Response New York with some fifteen-million dollars sent to us from Lutherans and others around the country and around the world. Through LDRNY we walked with the victims of 9/11 and their families, accompanied the economic victims of this tragedy, provided respite for pastors and teachers, and counseling for children, and pursued many other opportunities for comfort and renewal. We formed a bridge with many partners—public, interfaith, ecumenical, private—and nurtured and supported associations for victim's families, "unmet needs tables," and more. I traveled around the country and to other countries, bringing a perspective from the ground in New York to the altered landscape of our world. That altered landscape, and our response to it as congregations and denominations, is the subject and purpose of this book.

Interfaith dialogue, communal worship, presence in the firehouses, conducting memorials and funerals, deep conversations about faith and doubt and the presence of God, explaining life on the ground to friends around the corner and around the world, became part of the fabric of every parish and pastor in our synod.

Several days after the tragedy almost every Lutheran pastor and many lay members of our congregations in our metropolis gathered with our national leaders at Holy Trinity on the West Side. After coming back from Ground Zero with our national leaders I told those assembled: We have been baptized for this moment.

Grace
After the attacks on 9/11, we continue to witness many ground zeros: Katrina, Sandy Hook, Ferguson, Paris, San Bernardino, Syria, Orlando, even the daily violence in the mean streets of America's broken cities. Natural disasters, often exacerbated by human failure, have struck as well: hurricanes, tsunamis, drought, floods, earthquakes, tornadoes. We in North America have experienced firsthand the fear, helplessness, and vulnerability many in the world experience every day. Every one of these crises has jolted me back to that beautiful September day, and every one of them stirs up in my heart the great longing people felt to be near us, to stand

with us, to do something tangible. In my longing to make a difference—and to ensure that my church makes a difference—in so many lives torn apart in places of hurt and hope around the corner and across the globe, I have realized deeply my own gratitude for the many ways love and grace closed the distance between us in the days after September 11.

Five years after the attacks, I wrote a book about the first chapters in this saga, *Grace All Around Us*, which explored my experience at the time, and honored my long love story with New York City. Until I moved back to Chicago to lead the domestic ministries of my communion, the Evangelical Lutheran Church in America (ELCA), I had lived in the New York metropolis my entire ministry. My first call in 1973 was to two congregations in Woodside, Queens, where I learned a little Spanish and directed youth ministry. I was called to a congregation in Jackson Heights, Queens in 1974 and served there for eight years. During my time in Jackson Heights we grew a church of many different ethnic groups, in many ways a typical New York story. Those were the years that my leadership became rooted in the discipline and arts of community organizing. In the 1980s I served a parish in Bergen County, New Jersey, while also serving as a consultant to community organizing efforts across the greater New York metropolitan area. For twelve years I served as bishop of the Metropolitan New York Synod of the ELCA, with over two hundred congregations throughout Long Island, the city of New York, and the Hudson Valley, who collectively worship in over twenty languages. My family has lived in Queens, in Manhattan apartments on the Upper East Side, in Union Square downtown and uptown in Harlem. I have always loved the city, but since September 11 that love continues to move me in ways I can hardly bring to words. In Scripture God's promises are made real in turf, God's faithfulness is expressed on the ground, in places of hurt and hope. The passion emanating from Ground Zero in New York has made it, for me, a kind of Holy Land. In Chicago, a city I love and embrace, my heart still burns with New York fire, especially every September as I remember that day.

One of my favorite books is Georges Bernanos' *Diary of a Country*

Priest. It records the thoughts of an ordinary parish priest, his struggles with the mundane, his relevance to the rhythm of life in his rural parish, his attempts to pray, his wrestling with faith and doubt. In it he faces his own death, even as he has helped others face their own living and dying. The priest loves his turf, even while seeing clearly its folly and faults. He loves the people he encounters, even those who vex and irritate him. *Grace All Around Us* was a kind of "diary of an urban bishop," looking at September 11 and its rippling effects through the eyes of a pastor called to be a bishop. It documented my own struggle between doubt and faith, the difficult effort to find a voice in which to pray in the shadow of Ground Zero. It was a journal of awe and respect for the many people whose faith and compassion have left their mark on me. At Ground Zero we learned from others who had gone through tragedy before us, and I pray that some insights we have gained may be helpful to others, and relevant at any moment of tragedy.

This book's title, *Baptized for This Moment*, is rooted in the shared experience of Christian congregations of many denominations as our world is constantly challenged and changed. This new book is about today, about living into that altered landscape, about the mission of the Church and its baptized disciples in God's movement of reconciliation and restoration through the death and resurrection of Jesus. Both books have been offered in the spirit of the last words of Bernanos' compelling novel. A parishioner records the last words of the dying priest: "He said, 'Does it matter? Grace is all around us.'"

Public Faith, Public Church

For many of us who were directly involved, the events of September 11 reframed our theology and reinvigorated our practice of ministry. Yet as a society, we Americans seem to have moved from lamentations and grief to hardened anger. This visceral, communal anger has come to define the discourse in the common spaces remaining in the public square. How does the grace of faithful people and institutions enter space so permeated with fear and anger? This present book is a call to do just that, to re-engage the soul of faith (and in particular the Abrahamic faiths—Jewish, Christian, Islam) in the public arena, to encourage congregations to accompany public society with the most graceful and irenic and communal commitments of our traditions. Religion is today sometimes being used to exclude, attack, judge, discriminate, dominate, denigrate. The towers fell by an act of those invoking the name of God. This book is a call, in the name of God, for congregations and other religious institutions to offer hospitality in an often alien world, to accept invitations to tables we have not set. The communal anger and fear around issues of interfaith presence, immigration, refugees, war and peace, race, justice, and poverty can only be faced with grace and courage in nascent relationships, at new communal tables, by growing in understanding and mutual respect. Faith can help frame and inspire these conversations, faith which goes public as we figure out how we must spend our energy, not inviting "in" but learning how to be invited "out." Our faith must lead us out into the world where people who are hurting need our help.

> Our faith must lead us out into the world where people who are hurting need our help.

In *Grace All Around Us* I wrote about the ways grief—personal and collective—drives us to seek the healing that liturgy and fellowship offer. The stakes are now higher. Acts of terrorism are no longer an exception. Climate change stirs devastating natural disasters. Unspeakable acts of violence erupt across America with disturbing frequency. Crises arise every day, everywhere. Our fearful reaction may cause us to lose our sense of hospitality, vote against our best interests, justify overt racism, collude in surrendering our civil liberties, and favor diverting dollars to war and incarceration instead of funding social safety nets. We are reluctant to admit that our way of life is causing damage to our planet that may not be fixable at any cost. Largely absent in our public discourse are the values that lie at the heart of our Abrahamic faith; finding the language and having the vision to embrace the poor and vulnerable, prioritizing peace and justice over security, seeking understanding, and giving way to Christ's radical call to love one another.

We find enormous strength and resilience within our collective faith heritages. But we must redefine, and refine, our respective theologies. I speak from within my Lutheran communion, in solidarity with Protestant mainline denominations and the western Roman Catholic tradition. For mainline denominations, this means coming to terms with how invested our institutions are in the status quo and looking for ways to articulate a broad, inclusive, mainline Christian polity that supersedes the increasingly petty denominational constructs we cling to. As we go forward together, can we build bridges with all who share our Abrahamic faith, bearing witness to the grace we find all around us?

I am sounding a practical call to everyone everywhere. How can pastors and the lay disciples in their congregations summon the courage to tackle uncomfortable conversations and confront difficult situations with the love and peace and faith we feel in God's graceful presence? Can we learn that politeness and true peace are two different things? How do we step out into wider worlds as a Church seeking hospitality and offering hospitality in turn to all, no matter what their religion, gender, ethnic background, economic circumstances or sexual orientation? How do we build public spaces and set new tables where everyone's gifts are needed and welcomed? What tools will help us ask the right questions, and to prefer meaningful questions over pat answers? How can we escape the cycle of anger, fear and scarcity thinking that ensnares us?

This book will take us from that archetypical event, 9/11, through natural disasters, through our sorry string of man-made catastrophes, to today, from numbness and anger and despair to understanding, acceptance, and fruitful collective action.

The bottom line of grace is abundant life. Christians experience tragedy through the lens of the ground zero of the paschal mystery: the death and resurrection of Jesus. The final chapter in this book offers the bottom line of *resurrection*. The grace all around us is the presence and promise of our Risen Lord. We Christians already know the end of the story, etched out in the details of our public struggle for the soul of the world. The grace all around us is eternal, accessible, and sufficient.

1. *Where were you, and what were you feeling on September 11, 2001? How did that day shape your world view? In what ways do you carry any feelings about that event with you?*

2. *What other local, national or world events have caused similar feelings?*

3. *In what ways do you recognize grace all around you? In what ways do you hinder or help grace in its work in the world? Give specific examples.*

4. *In response to traumatic events, whether experienced first-hand or not, how does your faith inform your reactions and how you process such events?*

CHAPTER TWO

FROM LAMENTATIONS TO ANGER TO COMFORT AND RENEWAL

How lonely sits the city that once was full of people! How like a widow she has become...is it nothing to you, all you who pass by? Look and see if there is any sorrow like my sorrow which was brought upon me...

Lamentations 1:1, 12

What the cutting locust left, the swarming locust has eaten. What the swarming locust left, the hopping locust has eaten, and what the hopping locust left, the destroying locust has eaten....lament like a virgin dressed in sackcloth for the husband of her youth.... The fields are devastated, the ground mourns; for the grain is destroyed, the wine dries up, the oil fails.

Joel 1:4, 8, 10

Lamentations: Building a House for Sorrow

The book of Lamentations begins with these words: "How desolate sits the city that once was full of people. How like a widow she has become." In the ancient world, cities were destroyed so often that a literary type emerged called "a lament over a fallen city." Once ancient lamentations are now modern: New York, Washington, Madrid, Paris, Brussels, Maiduguri, Beirut, Baghdad, Damascus, Juba, Ferguson, Baltimore, Chicago, New Orleans, Mogadishu, St. Paul, Baton Rouge, Dallas, Nice, Istanbul...

In October of 2001 Kathleen O'Connor gave an eye-opening lecture on the Book of Lamentations at Boston University. She said, "This book is 'a house for sorrow,' as Alan Mintz aptly calls it." In the lecture she connected the time of Lamentations to the September 11 attacks. "Jews read it on the 9th of Av to commemorate two historic destructions of Jerusalem and their long history of suffering. After September 11, Lamentations belongs to us all."

The destruction of Jerusalem in 587 BC was the catastrophic ground zero for ancient Israel. Most scholars place Lamentations in the context of this annihilation, exile and spiritual devastation. It gathers the many voices of the survivors of the city's fall into a primal scream. The voices we hear even to this day give competing opinions about the disaster. They are united in pain. To find a voice, to insist on saying what happened and how it feels, to go deeply into the pain and utter it in language is not only soul-crushing work; it is, paradoxically, a beginning of hope and a restoration of the dignity of human agency. And, as Lamentations makes vividly clear, it takes three voices to make a lament. There are the voices of the wounded and devastated of Jerusalem, personified in the book as Daughter Zion: bereft, violated, widowed, and abandoned. There is the voice of the narrator, the one who listens. There is the voice of God: silent.

If the voice of wounded Daughter of Zion cannot or will not speak, then grief becomes hopelessness, bitterness, dehumanizing spiritual death. The sufferer becomes an object, not subject of her history. When disaster strikes, denial of pain and strategies of anesthetized disengagement are ways to survive. When the denial becomes routine, when we are stuck in ossified post-traumatic strategies, we become locked in a house of despair, when what we need is to create a house for our sorrow. When tragedy strikes, at some point, we must name it and cry out in our pain.

If the narrator does not show up, Lamentations cannot be expressed. If the narrator is just a narcissistic voyeur, then the Daughter of Zion is still alone, even amid a crowd. But if the narrator is able to be changed, moved to compassion, able to feel his or her own pain as a birthplace of spiritual solidarity, then two begin to build the house for sorrow.

While a glint of hope breaks forth in the third of the five poems of Lamentations, it is only a faint reminder of God's presence and promises. Mostly the voice is silent. The more insistently those who lament demand God's attention, the more pervasive the silence. Kathleen O'Conner told us: "Had the poets of Lamentations given speech to God, God's words would silence debate. The struggles with pain would come to closure prematurely. Any words from God would trump all speech. Instead, God's silence honors voices of suffering. It gives reverence to anger and resistance, to tears and despair. It lingers over what we in this culture so thoroughly deny." And it is precisely to linger and remain present in our pain that is counter-cultural today. We want only quick or easy solutions in our age of impatience, flitting from one thing to the next, looking for a quick and final fix in a single revolution of the news cycle. There are so few spaces for Lamentation in our time.

The two voices in Lamentations weave about throughout the poems, in the context of the silence. The narrator moves from third person observer to first person partner with the Daughter of Zion. At first the narrator impersonally judges: "Jerusalem sinned grievously, so she has become a mockery; all who honored her despise her, for they have seen her nakedness; she herself groans, and turns her face away." (1:8) The one who suffers is an object. The narrator offers bogus conclusions, like the friends of Job. The narrator usurps God's voice and tacks on simplistic religious explanations or happy little endings. But the narrator keeps listening, keeps showing up, keeps crying out: "Is it nothing to all you who pass by?"

Notice what happens as space for Lamentation opens up. In the persistent listening the narrator stops talking about the Daughter of Zion in the third person and speaks directly to her. "What can I say to you, to what compare you, O daughter Jerusalem? To what can I liken you, that I may comfort you, O virgin daughter Zion?"(2:13) Finally, the narrator is moved to cry out to God with the Daughter of Zion. "She," "I," and "You," have become "Us," "We." "Remember, O Lord, what has befallen us: look, and see our disgrace! We have become orphans, fatherless...Restore us to yourself, O Lord, that we may be restored; renew our days as of old—unless you have utterly rejected us, and are angry with us beyond measure." (5:1,3,21,22) The Daughter of Zion and the narrator share and feel the pain together. They cry out together. They question together. Together they hurl their lamentations against the silence and wait on the Lord in solidarity with those who cry out, "My God, why?"

> The first order of business in any private or communal tragedy is building the house for sorrow, attending to Lamentations.

What lesson is to be drawn by congregations trying to respond in faith and love to crises of all kinds, whether natural or caused by human hands? It is that the first order of business in any private or communal tragedy is building the house for sorrow, attending to Lamentations. In eighteen group conferences after the September 11 attacks I heard pastors and lay people give voice to their sorrow, their anger, their stories. Receiving the lament of the community is soul searing work. O'Conner says about Lamentations: "Lamentations encourages a religious attitude of openness not to what is beautiful and nourishing in the world, as do so many contemporary spiritualities. It calls us to name, attend to, and to lament what is devastating and brutal, anything that prevents the full flourishing of life on this planet. This is a time to pay reverent attention to every genuine sorrow." All the woeful burdens we carry are unpacked and sorted out in the stories we tell. People from across the country and around the world took on the ministry of the narrator and listened to us, thereby helping us build the house for our sorrows.

It is the way of the world to look away once our curiosity is satisfied, our horror aroused, once we have achieved our private catharsis. Have many of our congregations not already forgotten the South Asian tsunami, and the battered communities and shattered lives in New Orleans and the Gulf Coast since Katrina? I visited Fukashima, Japan in 2012, the year after the earthquake and tsunami. I witnessed very little public acknowledgment of what happened amid the torn landscape, the mile after mile of destruction. The Japanese quietly rebuilt their lives and faced their losses in isolation from a world with a short attention span. Lamentations takes time, sustained attention, loving proximity. The world may tell us it's time to move on after tragedy strikes, but God does not *move on*, God *moves in*, deeper and deeper into the tragedy, and our response to tragedies of every sort must first take the form of lament. Comfort will come after the lament (Second Isaiah 62:4, "You shall no more be termed Forsaken...") but initially grace all around us sounds like uncontrolled weeping.

Everyone who draws breath has ground zeros in their lives. A nine-year-old Syrian refugee lies alone, dead on a beach. The whole world turns toward this image in horror, becomes the narrator of this lamentable tragedy. Then terror in Paris, San Bernardino, Brussels, Orlando, Nice. More lamentation, tragedy, fear. How easily our lamentation may turn to anger, to xenophobia, to talk of walls, to racial and religious profiling. The public space for building a house for sorrow, for lament, gone. Consider how quickly we left that Syrian boy and the grief of his family, alone on the beach.

And yet, the Church is constantly called to that space, as we are called to persevere in Hebrews 10: 24-25: "Let us consider how to provoke one another to love and good deeds, not neglecting to meet together, as is the habit of some, but encouraging one another." We are called to continue to ask one another how we are doing in those places where sorrow has had its way. When tragedy strikes in any form, let us pick up our lives and move forward into God's future. We Christians cannot avert our eyes from desolation, nor let the short attention span of today's culture move us on too quickly from the small and large disasters that traumatized our fragile world. "Lamentations," according to Kathleen O'Conner, is an act of resistance. It teaches us to lament and to become agents in our relationship with God, even if our fidelity only takes the form of telling God and one another our truth.... Lamentations crushes false images, smashes syrupy pictures, destroys narrow theologies. It pours cold water upon theologies of a God who prospers us in all things, on a God who cares only about us, on a God who blesses our nation and punishes our enemies, as if we were God's only people."

Our lamentations are not the isolation and depression of wounded entitlement or private grief, but the community at the foot of the cross moving outward in solidarity and love toward the sorrow of the world.

The Knock on the Door: Enabling Genuine Love

Kathleen O'Connor pointed out: "To honor pain is not an invitation to solipsism, narcissism or egocentric foolishness. To honor pain means to see it, acknowledge its power, and to enter it as fully and squarely as we can, perhaps in a long spiritual process. To do so is ultimately empowering and enables *genuine love, action for others,* and *true worshipfulness.*"

For many throughout the world, lamentations are part of the fabric of everyday life. About a month after the September 11 tragedies I joined a group of local ecumenical leaders at the national headquarters of the Episcopal Church in the United States on 2nd Avenue to welcome an international ecumenical delegation, "A Living Letter of Compassion to U.S. Churches." They came from places where insecurity, violence, and tragedy are common—Pakistan, Palestine, Indonesia, among other nations—and they shared many of their stories. Hearing their voices was crucial, for without the narrator there can be no lamentations.

When the conversation with our visitors from the World Council of Churches turned political I learned how lamentations enable *genuine love.* I became agitated. I did not want to hear why people hated America or what could possibly justify this mass murder in our city. Not yet. It seemed that these visitors, the "narrator" of our lamentations, were still observing our sorrow in the third person mode, passing judgment, not really seeing us. I was still lamenting. When it was my turn to speak I said: "We are just so sad right now. We can still smell our brothers and sisters in the rubble downtown. We are not ready for lectures. Please, just sit down with us and share this time when our faces are in the dust. My head tells me you are probably right and we have a lot to learn and we need to address our global politics. My heart is not ready."

I rose to leave. One of the delegation, Bishop Dandala, the Methodist bishop of South Africa, asked me to wait. He allowed my lamentations to enable genuine love. This dear, wise man said something like this: "In our culture when tragedy happens we don't all visit at once. We come a few at a time so that each time the person in sorrow has to answer the door and tell the story again of what happened and shed the tears. As the story is told again and again healing can begin. We will keep knocking on your door. We will not leave you alone in your grief..." That is how genuine love shows up. Cards, letters, visits, money gathered and sent, emails, stuffed animals, visits, all of these signs of genuine love sustained those of us at Ground Zero in our lamentations. Genuine love checks in from time to time. Genuine love does not say, "It's time to move on" until healing has begun. And genuine love is this: to speak the truth in love, but only so much truth as the wounded can bear. Genuine love is to sit down in the dust with the other, to be silent, to listen, to speak the healing word only when God puts it in your mouth.

> Genuine love is to sit down in the dust with the other, to be silent, to listen, to speak the healing word only when God puts it in your mouth.

Many years after the tragedy in New York I am still answering the door (especially at each 9/11 anniversary) and knocking on other doors, lamenting other conflicts, other tragedies, hearing sad stories and telling our own.

When You Knock on the Door

The lessons drawn from 9/11 and other crises we have witnessed, both natural and of human origin, can help us formulate some useful guidelines to help congregations respond to public disasters around the world or around the corner.

- *Reach out immediately and tangibly.* This is the "knocking on the door" that the member of the World Council of Churches delegation was talking about when he said that we begin to heal each time we answer the door and tell someone what happened. Lamentations enabling genuine love looks like: phone calls, letters, emails, flowers or other things we send as a way of sending something of ourselves when tragedy strikes. Lamenters hang on to these concrete signs of solidarity.

- *Establish as soon as possible the appropriate channel for gifts.* Tragedy and disaster evoke visceral responses. We want to respond. There are a lot of opportunists and bottom feeders out there. For Lutherans, the Lutheran Disaster Response is the gold standard. Get the contact information in front of people immediately. In the case of communal tragedies, such as the shootings in Ferguson, Charleston, Baltimore, Baton Rouge, St. Paul, Dallas, and others, have your congregation work closely with the national and local church body leaders and ecumenical groups.

- *If possible, send money.* In the immediate hours and days after a disaster, flexibility is everything. Money enables immediate and appropriate responses. We live in a culture in which many people like to make a "designer response," in other words to meet their own needs rather than the needs on the ground. Used clothing, truckloads of Bibles, stuffed animals have their place, but initially those responding need to get what they need when they need it and that means: Send money. Send it to appropriate networks. Send it as well to local expressions of the Church. That often means the offices of the local bishop, president, or presbyter. They are well equipped to coordinate and match needs and resources. Resources may overflow into (and even overburden) individual congregations good at telling their story, while less media-savvy congregations with even greater needs may depend heavily on the solidarity of the collective Church body.

• *Make sure any personal visit is timely and appropriate.* Stay away until you are needed or invited. Bishops in New Orleans and the Gulf Coast spoke of people who showed up with truckloads of redundant materials wanting to be housed and fed, taxing an already strained infrastructure. People descended on our office in New York after 9/11 unloading all kinds of things—much of it unneeded—and expecting hospitality and a tour of Ground Zero before we had even caught our breath. Sometimes of those who reached out to us grew irritated if emails or voicemails went unanswered. Remember that when tragedy strikes, people on the ground will be running hard. We did value "knocks on the door," of all kinds, and every message we received brought hope. Later, when I had a chance, I tried to answer every phone call and email, and personally thanked everyone who sent anything. But put your need to be recognized or thanked low on your list of expectations as you respond to the crises of others.

• *If you have a skill or vocation which is relevant to first response then visit as soon as possible.* Trained counselors, rescue workers, disaster response leaders, those experienced in "defusing" traumatic experiences of first responders, experienced disaster response experts, construction and iron workers (if relevant to rescue and recovery) and other needed responders are usually most welcome.

• *Arrange opportunities for people to gather for prayer and spiritual comfort.* Open up spaces for lamentation, for people to take their questions and their doubt their sorrow, spaces for rekindling of hope and solidarity.

• *Be persistent.* Check in with victims regularly in the months and years ahead. If you don't "move on," the message is clearly conveyed that God's presence and compassion will also not "move on" until healing is well begun.

• *At the right time, visit.* Following the initial energy (and even euphoria) of attending to a disaster or tragedy, depression, spiritual enervation and physical exhaustion may set in for those on the front line. A timely visit from the outside world can be an occasion for renewal of spirit. But don't become a burden. Make you own hotel and travel arrangements rather than expecting to be put up.

• *Don't forget care and respite for the caregivers.* Offer vacation homes to pastors and chaplains and first responders. If you are a pastor, offer to use your vacation to visit and preach at a congregation in a disaster area and give local clergy a badly needed break.

• *Listen before you begin to articulate your faith.* When you mail, email, phone or visit, always first ask, "How are you doing?" And listen. Repeated articulation of lament is the path to healing. Share your faith in a way that does not shut off expressions of doubt, anger or sorrow by the victims. Always place the hands of those affected by tragedy into the hands of the ultimate Visitor.

Ramallah: Enabling Action for Others

In an upper room in Ramallah several years ago a Muslim sharia judge helped me to continue to heal from the trauma and loss of the 9/11 tragedy in New York. I was with a delegation of Lutheran Church leaders and our presiding bishop to show support for the Lutheran and ecumenical Christian Church in Palestine, visit their ministries in schools and refugee camps, negotiate with Israeli leaders around the Augusta Victoria Hospital tax issues, and share interfaith and ecumenical conversations. We had met Yassir Arafat, Mohammed Abbas, President Moshe Katzav of Israel and other political leaders. In Ramallah we walked up at least five flights of stairs and emerged into the offices of the chief Palestinian judges of sharia law. They were dressed in red-lined turbans and flowing robes. We sat in a circle and listened as one of the judges address us in Arabic, translated by Bishop Munib Younan of the Lutheran Church in Palestine. He began by telling of the frustration of Muslims who have been unable to reach the holy places in Jerusalem during the occupation. He cited the Omar Covenant of 638 AD in assuring Bishop Younan that Christians would have equal rights with Muslims in the Palestinian constitution. Then he mentioned 9/11.

"We have suffered much because of 9/11," he said. All during this trip my internal antenna rose at every mention of the events of September 11. Jews and Muslims, diplomats, political and ecumenical leaders were all using the "9/11 changed everything" mantra in their political analysis and assorted primal screams. When the judge said that 9/11 was a cause of their suffering I took him on. I interrupted him: "I'm from New York, sir. 9/11 isn't just a slogan, a way of talking about politics, or a vessel to fill with your own meaning. It changed our world too, it happened to us. Thousands died and we are only beginning to feel their pain." I spoke of the misinterpretation of Islam that we were trying to combat, that somehow there was an Islamic justification for this mass murder. "You, sir, are a religious leader, a scholar of Koran, a theologian. We have spent a lot of effort to defend your beautiful religion. I want to know what your scripture, your faith, what you personally have to say about what happened in New York."

He became emotional. He spoke with a quavering voice. "Islam forbids such killing! It calls us to protect souls and lives. Islamic law leads us to work for one understanding, love, security, peace, dignity." He quoted a line from one *sura* of the Koran: "the taking of one life is the taking of every life; the saving of one soul is the saving of every soul." He spoke of his hopes for peace and his compassion for the people of New York. I was stunned to silence. I choked back tears. This was the first time I had heard a Muslim leader unequivocally condemn our communal tragedy on September 11. He said nothing about why America is hated, or any other rationale. Just, "We condemn." Later a journalist on our trip said to me that the judge must have been waiting to say this to someone. It was direct and primal, from the heart.

Lamentations *enabled action for others* in two ways. Although New York was heavy on my mind, I was in the Holy Land to help build another house of sorrows. We spent our time listening to the laments of Israelis who had endured terror attacks. With the many spontaneous shrines, candles and pictures which I saw spring up in Union Square weighing on my heart, I could readily enter into the shrines marking scenes of violence and death at bus stops and markets in Jerusalem. We spoke with many in the West Bank refugee camps who had lost loved ones in the Israeli suppression of the intifada. People took us through piles of rubble and showed us where their families had lived before their homes were destroyed. People invited us into their homes, gave us tea and spoke of their losses and suffering. It seemed such a small thing to listen but the gratitude expressed to us for taking time and keeping company, I will never forget. And so as both the narrator and the Daughter of Zion in this particular lament, I entered a space where I was able to grow into wider worlds, wider understanding, deeper empathy. I think that this is how it worked for the judge. He knew we were there listening. Maybe our presence as companions to their lamentations opened up space for him to say things he could never say politically in the midst of the conflict. To be able to lament ends the time of the paralysis of despair. The defiant act of naming the sorrow is the prelude for action in wider arenas of this world's sorrow.

We must all, I think, confront our own religious traditions, the sorrows we have caused in the past, before we can explore the possibilities our faith offers to build houses of sorrow as foundations for even greater habitations of justice, mercy, and love. Islam, Judaism and Christianity co-exist today in both relational and disparate forms. We must give one another our best, most irenic responses, not the worst or skewed or self-serving responses to this deeply challenging world. The president of Israel, Arafat, Abbas and a sharia judge all spoke of the changing world. Our visits to them were relevant and welcome precisely because we were offering no *Realpolitik* but were mere pilgrims for peace, willing to be in conversation, listening to their pain and hope in our own hearts. We Christians were there at an historical time (the Israeli Knesset had just voted in favor of the "roadmap for peace" the second night of our visit) with nothing to give but the wisdom and passion of our sorrow, our bottom line faith in the Prince of Peace. As we know today that "roadmap" continues to be a "road not taken" in the midst of the ongoing conflict in the Middle East. But religious institutions must understand that the day approaching, which anchors and orients our peacemaking efforts, is also a long game this side of heaven.

> The defiant act of naming the sorrow is the prelude for action in wider arenas of this world's sorrow.

Enabling True Worshipfulness

On the one year anniversary of the 9/11 attacks I was about to cross the George Washington Bridge at the exact hour of the day when the first plane hit the towers. WQXR radio station played "Lachrymosa" (Tears) from Mozart's *Requiem*. I crossed the bridge and let my tears mingle with those of the metropolis. Communal lamentations. In that year lamentations took many forms, from silence and tears to tales of death and heroism and rescue, to morbid thoughts about the future, to repeated expressions of abandonment. Sometimes they were enclosed in prayers, other times at the shaking of the fist at God. The question, "Where was God on September 11?" was not only on the cover of Time magazine, but in the laments of many and lamentations also arose in music and liturgy.

I remember leading worship at New Hope, a storefront church near Yankee Stadium in the South Bronx. Most of the members are either in recovery or family members of those living one day at a time. Most are also materially poor. The congregation was about to begin a time of extended prayer and laying on of hands for healing before the liturgy of Holy Communion. I blurted out to the pastor, "I'm standing in the need of prayer." The past week I had received an unnerving medical diagnosis. "For what should we pray?" he asked me and I whispered to him my lamentation. The congregation then did for me what they do for one another every Lord's day. The prayer deacons stood at the altar. Those asking for prayer and anointing for healing came forward to kneel. I knelt with other brothers and sisters. I felt hands on my head. They asked me to speak my pain, and I was able to say, "I'm sick and I'm afraid." Around me others were telling their stories, giving voice to their lamentations. The jazz and Gospel ensemble moved from "Precious Lord, Take My Hand," to "Coney Island Jesus," (composed by the bassist, who had experienced conversion and the beginnings of healing from drug addiction on the beach at Coney Island). There were tears, emotional prayers. The room was noisy with the clamor of lamentation and prayer. The hands on my head were strong, the voices prayed for ten minutes, some in charismatic language I had never heard. They were not able to mitigate my diagnosis or dispel all of my fear, but I rested in the community of Jesus and in the promises of God.

The time of prayer and communal lament was then brought to the altar with bread and wine and all was transformed by the presence of Jesus, crucified and risen, at Holy Communion. My world was in the Eucharist, and the Eucharist inhabited my world. After that liturgy I was able to begin to face the future, for I had given voice to my sorrow and my fear.

Here must be the first response of the Church in the face of any of the tragedies we now find afflicting us: Show up. Listen. Tell stories. Pray. Here is the promise of Joel: lamentation enables true worshipfulness. "*I am sending you grain, wine, and oil, and you will be satisfied*" (2:19). Not now. Not yet in our time of lamentations. But it will come.

1. *Where does hope "leak out" in your community? Have you ever been surprised in finding hope in the midst of despair? Describe what happened.*

2. *How do you balance remembering with moving on? Share a story if you can. In what ways does your congregation remember while still leaning into the resurrection promise that defines the Church?*

3. *How would you describe genuine love? When you see genuine love, how do you recognize it? Give some examples.*

4. *List three obstacles to the Church expressing genuine love.*

5. *How do you identify true worshipfulness? What does that look like in your congregation?*

CHAPTER THREE

PUBLIC CRISES, PUBLIC RE-ENCHANTMENT

The fate of our times is characterized by rationalization and intellectualization, and, above all, by the 'disenchantment of the world.' Precisely the ultimate and most sublime values have retreated from public life either into the transcendental realm of mystic life or into the brotherliness of direct and personal human relations.

Max Weber

September 11, 2001, Noon
This morning we watched in horror from our 16th floor office windows as both towers lit up, then fell into a cloud of smoke and ash. We are now in the chapel of the Interchurch Center in Morningside Heights, and I am facing hundreds who have gathered to pray. For the previous hour we had been doing what millions did throughout the metropolis, trying to track down loved ones working in lower Manhattan. We called the offices of people we know from our synod who work in the area. I spoke to a panicked receptionist for a law firm a block away from the towers. We prayed togeth-

er on the phone. Now the chapel is filled with people still not knowing the fate of loved ones, and people unable to get home. I ask people to speak aloud the names of those for whom they are concerned.

Ortega y Gasset, the Spanish philosopher, said, "History happens when the sensitive crown of the human heart inclines to one side or the other of the horizon." That inclination of the human heart describes the context of our mission today.

I heard a changing America and its new history unfold, as the chapel rang out with the names of loved ones, spoken through clenched teeth, strained and breaking voices. Names of workers in Lower Manhattan, fire and police personnel, children in school, friends visiting. "Where's Rachel?" I hurled at God, joining those speaking names. In the litany of names I heard our communal movement from security to insecurity; from entitlement to vulnerability; from the comfortable veneer of our secularity, our disenchantment, to a yearning to speak to our Maker; from insularity to solidarity. What has always been just beyond the horizon, bubbling beneath the surface, began to come into view. Everything has changed. Nothing has changed. Everything is connected. Nothing is connected. Where's Rachel? Where's God? Where's my neighbor? Where is the safe place now? What the hell happened to us?

Helter-skelter

The great mysteries of existence were staring us in the face, the crown of our human hearts inclining toward a new horizon. David Tracy, writing about 9/11, said, "Before faith, hope, love you must know *finitude* (all these falling bodies, endless memorial services), *contingency* (I survived in my fire house, eleven brothers didn't), and *transience* (the empty sky downtown)." The Bible became very relevant because it talks to us about these primal things and about the horizon facing all of us: death. In the helter-skelter moments when death rained down on New York, the reflexive responses were almost invariably spiritual. Sitting on a bench next to a soot-covered survivor who is screaming hysterically as bodies rain from the sky, a pastor's wife who made it out of Tower One takes her hand and quotes Romans 8: "Nothing can separate us from the love of God in Christ Jesus, our Lord." One of our chaplains, who had run across the Brooklyn Bridge to the towers, anointed with oil firemen rushing into the building, a cruciform reminder of our baptism. Those descending the towers noted the glistening foreheads rushing past them to the rescue. Amandus Derr, the pastor of St. Peter's Lutheran Church heard one of these stories of ascent and descent, rescue and dying, from a member of his congregation. He shared it on Friday, September 14, at a noonday liturgy in the church's midtown Citigroup Center location. Hundreds heard him speak of Jacob's ladder, with angels ascending and descending. God is at both ends of the ladder, receiving those ascending home, present with those descending to earth.

On the street outside after that liturgy someone came up to me and asked me to pray for him. He was a Delta pilot who had flown in the first plane allowed back into New York airspace. He spoke of the fear and sadness besetting pilots and attendants. What had been a good, safe place—the airplane—was now a place of fear and a reminder of brutal tragedy. After my prayer he looked at me and smiled: "You look like you could use a prayer." He then placed his hands on my head and prayed for almost five minutes. That's how it was in those first days, enchantment rippling out, washing over the metropolis, spontaneously, fervently. You remember, don't you, wherever you were that day? We wanted to do two things. We wanted to be together, and we wanted to pray.

At ground zero, breathing lightly through my mask, I contemplated the rubble and groped for something, anything, to give me consolation. There is no happy little ending one can tack on. I stared at the obscene pile, pictures of loved ones in my mind buried there and I grasped desperately for any shred of what I thought I knew.

In the helter-skelter of this disaster, Scripture—itself honed in catastrophe and abandonment—came alive and continued to speak to the crown of any inclined human heart. Our hearts were broken, yes, but they were broken open.

Drawn to the Light

September 11, late evening: A member of one of our congregations, a part of the massive exodus from Ground Zero through Manhattan, made it safely home to her apartment in the South Bronx. Tired and covered with soot, numb with what she had seen and experienced, she encountered many neighbors in front of her apartment. They were in shock, like the Emmaus disciples, sad and puzzled and feeling like the ground beneath them had shifted. She said, "I'm not just going to stand here." She went up to her apartment and got a candle, brought it back to the street in front of her apartment and invited her neighbors to join her in prayer. They sang, "Precious Lord, take my hand..." They prayed fervently and publicly, as did millions around the world. They gathered every night for two weeks. Those in the neighborhood who went to Ground Zero every day for rescue and recovery told those gathering each night: "Please don't stop doing this. I can stand being down there if I know you are praying for us." Throughout the metropolis and the nation and world the "enchantment" bubbling beneath the surface of life broke forth. We gathered instinctively to pray, in the broadest possible way. Imams and rabbis and bishops and pastors and neighbors and strangers joined hands and hearts to pray. We saw our context etched out in the many flickering candles. St. Augustine is right. Our existence is anchored in our spiritual DNA. The soul is made for God and will never find its rest until it rests in God.

> St. Augustine is right. Our existence is anchored in our spiritual DNA. The soul is made for God and will never find its rest until it rests in God.

What we were seeing is manifestation of a turnaround by secularization theorists. In the more militantly secular versions of eighteenth-century Enlightenment and up through recent times, it was thought that secularization was the wave of the future. As the world became more modern that is, secular, religion would become irrelevant or totally a private affair.

Cribbing from Schiller, Max Weber saw the future as the "disenchantment" of the world. Instead, what we saw breaking out around the globe on the evening of 9/11 was nothing entirely new, but rather acts transfigured now in their intensity, and manifested in their overt expression. Nothing is the same. Everything is the same. We are witnessing a resurgence of religion around the world with all the cultural and political consequences attending to it. This is the reality examined by Samuel Huntington in his classic thesis "Clash of Civilizations," in which he posits that cultural and religious differences would become the principal source of conflict in the post-Cold War world. September 11 turned a bright and enduring light on the "re-enchantment" and "desecularization" of world history, on an abiding human hunger for spiritual meaning, connection and company, for holy comfort, for God. It also shed light on the power of religion to express hatred, settle scores, seed terror, and stoke xenophobia.

Spaces for enchantment opened up, or were revealed in New York, under the harsh light of the September 11 tragedy. We were awash in liturgy and scripture, in houses of worship and on the very streets of the city.

The Bible came alive in new ways. Pastor Richard Michael of Trinity Lutheran Church in Staten Island wrote this in the bulletin announcements the Sunday after 9/11:

> "We now seem to have joined the ranks of those who know "poverty" in a way we have not experienced it ever before. There have been wars, depressions, and tragedies, but this one somehow is different. Our "feet of clay" are exposed. We are still reeling from the blow. No matter the cries of our determination to overcome the enemy. This time the blow has staggered us. We shout "God bless America," but in the same breath must ask how the loss of thousands of lives can be a blessing? What must God have been thinking? There is our humanity waiting for us. We are a people of great wealth and resources who for a moment have the opportunity to join Lazarus in a beggar's view of the world. We

can learn an incredible lesson from down here about values and priorities, about needs and wants, about the view of much of the rest of the world of us. It is an opportunity the rich man in the parable did not have until it was too late. One scholar calls this view of the world, "the wisdom of the poor." If we can grasp this wisdom, perhaps we will alter our prayer from "God bless America," to "God make America a blessing to all the nations of the world."

In a sermon on 9/11, the Rev. Dr. James Forbes, Jr., Senior Minister Emeritus of the Riverside Church in New York, reflected on the image of people streaming from Ground Zero, from the city and declared: "We're all poor now." He then shared what millions of us came to lament, that this shared solidarity of poverty and vulnerability did not translate into greater global communal purpose. Instead it drove us to war. We are still living in that breach of shattered solidarity.

Classic works of visual art took on a new relevance. Bishop H. George Anderson went to Ground Zero with us, then reflected on this experience in a sermon preached September 23, 2001 at the chapel of Trinity Seminary, Columbus, Ohio. Speaking of rescue workers at Ground Zero, he said:

"As I saw their faces afterward, I recalled a fresco by Piero della Francesca depicting the resurrected Christ. From a distance the composition of the fresco is clearly triumphant. Soldiers lie sprawled in the foreground. The risen Christ steps out of the sepulcher, one foot resting on its lid; a banner of victory in one hand forms the apex of the composition. But as you get closer, you notice Christ's eyes—hollow, wary, staring as though they are running recaps of what he has just seen and done. This is truly the face of God, who has overcome evil—not by crushing it, but by enduring it and outliving it."

We mourned the dead and comforted the living. On September 25 I conducted, with two other pastors and a Jesuit priest, an ecumenical service for the employees and staff of American and United Airlines in remembrance of the four crews who died in the hijacked planes. The liturgy continued around the coffee urn and on the street outside the church as hundreds of uniformed airline pilots and staff gave voice to their lamentations.

We prayed ourselves into spiritual solidarity and refocused our collective mission. On September 23 we gathered all the pastors and hundreds of members of our Lutheran churches in the metropolis with our national leaders and regional bishops at Holy Trinity on the West Side. When we sang: "My Lord, What a Morning," we craned our necks to catch a glimpse of the promised new dawn on the edge of our darkness. Prayer, scripture, sober reflections, and music carried us forward.

Immigration spurs the re-enchantment of our country. The crowds at New York's annual worship for Lutherans from Guyana fill two churches to capacity. We conduct ecumenical and interfaith memorials in our metropolis for Guyanese, Latino, Tamil, Arab, Chinese, and East African victims of 9/11.

Music became an especially potent form of re-enchantment. Alex Ross, in *The New Yorker*, in the October 8, 2001 issue, remembers that on May 7, 1915, the day the Lusitania was sunk by a German torpedo, Charles Ives was standing on an elevated train platform when he heard a barrel organ playing *In the Sweet Bye and Bye*. One by one, those around him began to sing along: first, a workman with a shovel, then a Wall Street banker in white spats, and finally the entire motley crowd. "They didn't seem to be singing in fun," Ives recalled, "but as a natural outlet for what their feeling had been going through all day long." Ives recorded the experience in his *Orchestral Set No. 2*, in a movement entitled "From Hanover Square North, at the End of a Tragic Day, the Voice of the People Again Arose."

The collective human heart moved from private, insular agony to communal expressions of grief and loss, solidarity and hope, in the days after this tragic attack. At Union Square nightly vigils included the lighting of candles, spontaneous singing of *God Bless America*, and *Amazing Grace*. At baseball stadiums around the country, usually raucous crowds raised their voices together in heartfelt renderings of *God Bless America*. The New York Philharmonic put together an impromptu performance of Brahms *German Requiem*. Bach cantatas and Bruce Springsteen's haunting *My City of Ruin* helped us remember that when words die behind clenched teeth music can help us shoulder the heaviest part of our burden.

Liturgy and spiritual responses broke out in the aftermath of tragedy. The response was visceral: people instinctively prayed communally and publicly. What was bred in the bone, the tides of our spiritual birthright, came out in percussive waves of civic and religious liturgy, song, ritual.

Liturgy and scripture bind the Christian community and its mission to the presence of God and the grace all around us.

Liturgy and scripture bind the Christian community and its mission to the presence of God and the grace all around us. Liturgy and scripture take up the ongoing work of lamentations. A third of the Psalms are laments. Liturgy and scripture undergird the compassionate mission of the Christian community as it participates in disaster response. And today, liturgy and scripture must propel the healing work of the Christian witness into wider worlds of justice and community renewal. As we lament and heal we begin to see connections between what happened to us and the ongoing suffering and tragedy all through history and all around the world. September 11 set a new context for Christian worship and mission. It is a call for re-enchantment, not just in the private, or liturgical realm of life, but in the public square, in the Church's public mission for the life of a world awash in anger, in an ethos of scarcity, in terror, injustice, racism, bigotry, political paralysis, and the godless appropriation of religion to wage war.

Take the A Train

Who would have thought I would catch a fleeting glimpse of the kingdom of God, years ago, in the bowels of New York City, aboard the A Train? Back in the 1970s, crowds, pushing, angry exchanges, delays, twinges of fear, and random violence comprised every commuter's daily routine. Even today everyone wears the "subway mask," that impassive glare which says, "leave me alone and I'll do the same to you."

But in the days after 9/11, see a lone man waiting on the platform, tapping his stick, eyes shrouded by dark glasses and apparent blindness. Another man, his head buried in the *Daily News* looks up, alerted by the tapping. From the midst of the dark tunnel comes the rumbling of an approaching train. Craning necks peering into the void are rewarded by a sliver of approaching light. The man with the cane wears a quizzical, anxious expression. The man with the *Daily News* looks intently into the onrushing light, then saunters over to the man with the cane.

"It's the A Train. You want it?"

The blind man nods gratefully. The doors open and release their hordes. I couldn't believe what I saw next. Usually people knock each other—handicapped, elderly, pregnant, no matter—into next week to get a seat. But today they wait. Firm hands grasp the blind man's arm and guide him onto the train, then others enter carefully. Several people simultaneously offer their seats, and he is guided to one. His self-appointed guardian, still clutching his paper, asks him what stop he wants, and hears "Columbus Circle." As the train arrives at the appointed stop people back up to make room, and the blind man is firmly and kindly guided off the train. As we pull away from the station I look through the dirty window to see him being led to the stairway.

As the train raced through the dark tunnel I thought about the blind man, about his faith in hands he could feel and voices he could hear, and about his own internal orienting giftedness. I thought about his courage venturing sightless into the hostile void with the unproven belief that help would arrive. I thought about how his presence had changed our subway car into a caring community—however fleeting. I thought about the mundane character of this uncommon grace—a touch, a voice, a proffered seat—like a cup of cool water from a Samarian well. And I thought that instead of breaking in, maybe the reign of God is breaking out in the dark, anonymous corners of the world. If we want to catch a glimpse of God, we must, as the song admonishes us, "Take the A Train."

I want you to hang on to that image as we explore how congregations and religious institutions, how every baptized disciple, can respond to crises in the public arena today.

A Brief Exegesis on Public Provocation

> **Let us hold fast to the confession of our hope without wavering,
> for he who has promised is faithful. And let us consider how
> to provoke one another to love and good deeds, not neglecting
> to meet together, as is the habit of some, but encouraging one
> another, and all the more as you see the Day approaching.**
> **Hebrews 10:23-25**

I have been digging into this text with people in every possible venue. When I ask people what words or ideas jump out at them, a majority of the responses are the same: the word "provoke." But the sense in Hebrews is not what usually comes to mind when we hear the word provoke: egging someone on to anger, inciting, aggressively causing a reaction. In fact, the Latin root *pro vocare* means to put a call in front of someone. And in this case the call is not to anger or reaction or retribution, but to "love and good deeds." It is a call to inspire one another to show up in this polarized and angry world with love and grace. Looking at this text, we can begin to trace what the public life and witness of religious institutions, congregations and individual believers could look like amid tragedies both natural and of our own manufacture. Like the blind man wandering onto the subway train, what hope do we carry into the darkness?

The exhortation to "hold fast the confession of hope without wavering" is as relevant today as it was to the audience of Hebrew Christians living in persecution and internal turmoil in Jerusalem. I don't need to recount in detail the decline of the mainline Christianity, the general retreat from church-going, the missing generation of young adults, the seeming cultural irrelevance of our dwindling congregations. It seems Max Weber is right, and "disenchantment" is our present and future. We know all that and live it every day. But there are still thousands of garden-variety congregations embedded in our communities and God isn't finished with them yet. Dietrich Bonhoeffer has said: "We must never be servile before the fact." We confess hope, not certainty. Yet hope is a powerful thing.

When you get off the bus in midtown Manhattan a sign above the door tells you to "wait for the light." But when you get off the bus on the Lower East Side the sign is also in Spanish and says *espere la luz.* In English, "wait" is not as rich, romantic, and forward-leaning as the Spanish *"esperar,"* which means to wait, hope, expect, and anticipate all at once.

Hope permeates all our encounters in the public arena—as advocates in speaking truth to power; in community organizing one-on-ones with our neighbors; in providing much-needed social services; in encouraging economic development ventures; in running food pantries; in planning and planting community gardens. Our most valuable commodity in these efforts is hope. Our conversations are about what a world imbued with the values of Jesus should look like. Hope blooms in all our conversations about values, vision, reconciliation, mutual respect, and concrete action. Hold fast. Keep hope alive. *Esperanza.*

The light for which we wait is Jesus Christ, "for he who promised is faithful." And we not only wait for the light, but hope for it, long for it, work toward it, and look for it. *Esperanza!* As Christians we wait, work, and look for the light—the light of Jesus born in Bethlehem, born each day into our hearts through baptismal remembrance, and the end-of-time light on the horizon for which we long. We venture out into public space as agents of that hope.

In our polarized world it is indeed a "provocation" to seek a welcome at the table of the other. To seek new space, new tables for hopeful conversations that take root beneath the communal anger and move toward honesty and true listening. It is a call for leaders in our congregations to agitate for the spiritual maturity and hopefulness of their members on their Monday morning missions into public space.

It is counter cultural to be artisans and seekers of human community. To meet together in real time, as well as virtual space. Jimmy Carter told those gathered at the dedication of the 100,000th Habitat for Humanity home that most people think that Habitat is mainly about the house. But Carter said that we live in a world where a person of privilege and a person in poverty never have to be in the same space, or have a conversation. Rich and poor can live their whole lives without managing to encounter one another, and usually do. The institutional Church has the enormous capacity to convene such encounters among strangers, to seek welcome at tables where we know little and maybe fear a lot. That is a powerful thing in this polarized time. Only in discovering community will we find the corporate courage to channel pervasive public anger into a collective vision of hope.

It is time for the Church based in grace to find its voice, to be a teaching Church, so that the world may know where we turn to find our hope, our trust, our only security, our deepest reason to exist. We have so few collective spaces left for mourning, for grief (which underlies anger), and so few windows into the lives of others we don't understand. Congregations can become those places. Congregations can fill those spaces. A colleague of mine once asked in a sermon if any of us would be Christians if all we had to go on were the images of Christianity we see and experience in the media. None of us would elect to be part of what is publicly portrayed as

> It is time for the Church based in grace to find its voice...so that the world may know where we turn to find our hope, our trust, our only security, our deepest reason to exist.

judgmental, divisive, seeking its own ends, violent, abusive, controlling, private, smug, and self-contained. We have to prove that this image of Church is not the reality. It is time for an Encouraging Church to go public.

One widely popular and variously attributed definition of life is "one damn thing after another." And then you die. But Paul's promise of encouragement "all the more as you see the Day Approaching" gives congregations a more hopeful view. The passion of this life is worth it. Time, history, is heading somewhere. There is a point, a purpose. In the paschal mystery of the death and resurrection of Jesus, God has entered history. We have a story we carry into the world. We join the story already being enacted in the world. The "Day Approaching" is the reconciliation, the final restoration of all creation. The God who made the world still loves it. This sweet old, fallen world is loved by God and therefore embraced by Christ's body in the world, by us. In the paschal mystery of the life, death and resurrection of Jesus, the reign of God is remaking the world. This world has been returned to us as the space for all of our vocations. Our lives take on meaning in the shadow of the Day approaching.

Congregations, religious institutions, Christians, and all people of good will, this is what we carry on our A Train: a vision of hope; a commitment to community; an ethos of encouragement; the power to provoke in public, in service to the Day Approaching.

Church, be what you are, but be it in public, and be it for the life of this world, and the world to come. Re-enchantment forges forth as we take the A Train home.

1. *How difficult is it for you to "show up" in meaningful ways when public tragedies strike? Why? In what ways does your congregation show up? In what ways might your congregation show up in ways that other institutions cannot?*

2. *Our experience with trauma—individually and collectively—colors and shapes our expressions of faith. How much or how little do fear and anger play a factor in your responses? What do fear and anger have in common? Explain your answers.*

3. *What role might liturgy have in helping victims and those who support them process and respond to traumatic events? Give an example of a liturgy that did that for you.*

4. *Define "provocation." Is public provocation a natural component of a life of faith? Why or why not, and if so, how so? How does a Church publicly provoke?*

5. *What are the things that make it difficult for you to "Take the A Train" with others? What do you need in order to feel invited to help?*

CHAPTER FOUR

PUBLIC CHURCH FOR THE LIFE OF THE WORLD

Now in Jerusalem by the Sheep Gate there is a pool, called in Hebrew Beth-zatha, which has five porticoes. In these lay many invalids—blind, lame and paralyzed. One man was there who had been ill for thirty-eight years.

John 5: 1, 2

When Fear and Anger Surround Lamentation

San Pedro Sula, Honduras

Led through the filthy streets by Rafael Malpica Padilla, who directs global missions for the ELCA, we entered a tiny home—bare, stark, without plumbing—and met Yolanda and her children. One son, about five or six, curls on her lap. Her two daughters are there, nine and eleven, and a cousin, ten. We are in San Pedro Sula, Honduras, the second most violent city in the world. Yolanda has just been deported from Mexico with three of her children after trying to reach the United States.

 She left because her life and that of her children had become untenable. She is in her forties, well educated, but had lost her job. She could not find another one. Unemployment has skyrocketed in their economy. She could no longer feed her children. The culture of violence in Honduras is stark and pitiless. Yolanda's older son Emilio was walking down the road with a girl when gang members walked up and killed her right in front of him. He was then caught between police, who wanted his testimony, and the Mara gang who demanded his silence. The government has taken a military approach to the gang problem, meeting violence with violence and extra-judicial murder. The gang threatened her son and then began to recruit her daughters. To resist this recruiting is often a death warrant. She paid the coyotes, who expedite illegal immigration to the U.S., $6,000, exhausting her life savings and borrowing heavily from family. The coyotes told the comforting lie: "This will be easy."

They went through Guatemala and into Northern Mexico. Walking for many days. The thirst, the heat ("*Muy calor!*" her son chimed in, sitting on her lap). They were kidnapped by the Gulf Cartel, aided by her coyote. They tied her son by his hands and feet.

"Don't do that to my child!" Yolanda yelled at them.

"Do you want to get shot? Shut up."

They then gave her son cigarettes and let him hold a gun. The kidnappers were between eighteen and twenty and apparently high on drugs. They sexually violated some of the other women they held hostage. Yolanda made her children leave the room when she described this to us. The violence and terror were constant. The kidnappers would put guns in people's faces, kick people. Yolanda and her children were held in a house in Tampico for a ransom—equivalent to $3,000 each. So many migrants interdicted in Mexico are commodified and become victims of traffickers. Some talked about hiding in a cave, about seeing cadavers left over from human organ trafficking.

Now Yolanda's telling of the tale escalated and she spoke rapidly. They escaped. A guard put his gun behind the sofa and the captive men rushed him and his associates while the leader was out. Yolanda was upstairs. Some in the group jumped from the window. She and her children were at a window when some of the men who had escaped came back for them. She dropped two of them out the window to rescuers waiting below. She and the other children jumped down and they all ran barefoot towards safety. They hid in a drug store. The local police came. But Yolanda recognized them, remembering they had brought pizzas to the kidnappers. The store owners hid them. Finally, immigration police came and took them into custody.

The detention in Tampico was bad but Tapachula, in the state of Chiapas, was the worst, as Yolanda describes: "Horrible. Dirty mattresses. Smelly. Only one lousy meal a day." A human warehouse, devoid of humanity. Yolanda somehow found the courage to stand up for those being abused, especially Guatemalans, who could not speak Spanish.

"We are human beings, treat us well," she demanded.

After six days there they were deported on a bus, back to the unspeakable violence of San Pedro Sula.

She described her life now: "We are living life on the run. My older son Emilio still lives with us and is still hiding from the gangs. The Mara are all around here. This neighborhood is a dividing line between two gangs. My children are traumatized. They have nightmares. I work as a domestic maid. I make $100 a month, which barely pays rent, electricity and water." She has only enough to scrape up one meal a day for her family. It has been four years since she lost her job.

Stories like Yolanda's would be repeated many times by those Hondurans willing to share their experiences with us. Poverty, no economic hope, extreme and constant violence pushed children and families to flee only to embark on a journey replete with violence, exploitation, and abuse. And in the end, they were caught and sent back to the very conditions threatening them in the first place.

And then Yolanda shared her faith.

"I am so grateful that my kids are in a Christian school. I am thankful to God that they are okay. I am at home." Her hand swept across the tiny, humble shack. "I am at peace in my home. I am grateful to *Casa Alianza* for all their help." (Counseling, case management, help with books and uniforms for school were the only follow up Yolanda received after getting off the deportee bus.)

"I am more than a sad case," she says.

She shared her incarnation theology: "My kids and I are precious to God. God is right here with us. Scripture says that foxes have holes, birds have nests, but Jesus didn't have a place to lay his head. He knows I am here, he knows my children. He will not abandon us. He has been where we are." She grasped her Bible. "All books inform us, but the Bible forms us."

She then expressed gratitude for our coming to be with her. She thanked us for listening, (a refrain we would hear repeated again and again). Rafael prayed with us all and blessed the home and family. The kids hugged us. Yolanda was in tears—a proud, wise, compassionate sister in Christ. As we left, Michele, Yolanda's oldest daughter, gave each of us a beautiful card she had made during our visit. The cards were red, with interwoven hearts and expressions of love. It was Valentine's Day.

In Lamentation there is the Daughter of Zion. There is the listening narrator. There is also the surrounding cacophony of paralyzing fear, anger and violence trying to silence the lamentation. Can we hear them in our public context in North America, in our own self-imposed wall of fear and anger?

Corpus Christi, Texas

We walked into a large assembly room at the Bokenkamp Children's Shelter run by Lutheran Social Services of the South in Corpus Christi and were greeted by over one hundred waiting children sitting around tables. They were between thirteen and seventeen years old and had been apprehended at the border in McAllen, Texas and were being processed to reunite with family and begin their asylum cases. They were all from the northern triangle of Central America: Honduras, Guatemala, El Salvador. Children like them had been crossing the border unaccompanied for four years, each year twice as many as the year before. This year over 70,000 would cross. Rafael offered a greeting from our group in Spanish. We then fanned out, going from table to table. Even with my bad Spanish, and the limited English of one of the staff who accompanied me, we were able to listen to the stories of many children. Our questions were basic: Where are you from? How long did it take you to get here? What was your journey like? How is it in this place? Where do you have family? The answers formed a very clear picture. The biggest reason they came here? *"Violencia."* The first person I listened to, a girl of thirteen, was very clear.

"The gang would have killed me if I stayed."

We heard stories of extortion, family members being killed, threats. We also heard that children come to reunite with family. To get a job. When we asked about what it is like in this place many smiled and gave the same answer. *"Securidad."* Safe, secure. Stories of their journey varied. They came by bus, by train (nicknamed *la bestia*, the beast), and their most frequent final destinations were: New York, Maryland, Los Angeles, Boston. We also heard Oklahoma, Iowa and many places along the East Coast. Earlier we had visited a group foster home for even younger unaccompanied migrant children. Rafael and I shared a moment of emotion: these children are the age of our grandchildren. One child summed up the experience. He showed us a picture he had drawn of his home.

"I miss my family," he said. "I don't know if they are okay. My brother was killed in front of my house."

Children like these, cowering in buses in Texas and Arizona, waiting to be transported to similar facilities, are surrounded by angry mobs screaming at them, blocking their passage, accusing these lambs of God of bringing AIDS, Ebola, crime, drugs, gang activity into our country.

I joined another group I was working with in Istanbul in viewing a film clip of an ISIS massacre of 3,000 young cadets, mostly Shiite, at an Iraqi Air Force base. The room went silent and tears flowed. The sounds of young men and boys pleading for their lives grew to be too much. A Shiite cleric got up, walked to the computer and turned off the display of the massacre. We were watching the dawn of ISIS.

Religious leaders from Iraq, Norway, and the United States have made a commitment to research the prospects for building peaceful relations among people and states experiencing conflict and violence and to work to normalize such work and dialogues. Through the Peace Research Institute Oslo (PRIO) and The Catholic University of America, a group of Sunni, Shiite, Christian, Turkmen and Kurdish religious leaders from Iraq met in Istanbul in an effort to generate religious dialogue and seek action together for peace. This was the first effort by the PRIO to create safe space for Iraqi religious leaders. In that room leaders were speaking frankly and with passion to one another. More than one made the point that right now, with extremism surfacing from all religions, we are in a struggle for the soul of our Abrahamic faiths. We were seeking to find together ways in which religious leaders can have an effective role in brokering peace, fostering coexistence, and initiating vital humanitarian responses in places like Syria, Iran, and Iraq.

Many of the dialogue participants shared stories of suffering, terror and death, particularly wrought by ISIS, in their drive to create an Islamic state across Sunni areas of Iraq and Syria. A woman at the table told stories of women being sold, thousands of young men killed and the demolition of buildings and infrastructure by ISIS. Christian leaders told of their diminished presence in Iraq and the region and pleaded with the religious leaders around the table to not stoke religious anger and violence toward others. We heard harrowing, horrific accounts of human suffering. Some members of the group had been forced out of their homes by ISIS fighters. They addressed their concerns in our meeting. But the fact that Sunni, Shiite, Christian, Turkmen and Kurdish religious leaders were gathered at the table was an amazing statement of faith. A group of Yazidi religious leaders were also invited to the meeting in Istanbul but unable to come. They were still reeling from the 2014 ordeal on Mount Sinjar, the execution-style massacre of thousands of men and the enslavement of their women, the destruction of their villages. They put their lament into a message to our group which began: "When the soul is destroyed without a sin and the land is usurped by force and people are displaced coercively, that is repugnant injustice." An aura of helpless anxiety and fear permeated the meeting. The paralysis of anger and violence touched everyone.

Detroit

There was a tinge of sadness and resignation in the room. Faith leaders, Syrian and Arab community leaders, non-profit agency leaders were gathered from seven communities across the United States to collaborate together on welcoming the anticipated 10,000 Syrian refugees President Obama had promised to resettle in the United States. Lutheran Immigration and Refugee Services convened this group to help in the formation of welcoming communities. These leaders were from the communities of highest Syrian and Arab population, and the most likely to welcome these new neighbors. I was there with our delegation from Chicago. The day before brought news of the attacks in San Bernardino, California, carried out by Arab neighbors who pledged allegiance to ISIS (the Islamic State). The pushback across America, coming on the heels of the Paris attacks, heated up the rhetoric of fear and anger, targeting Muslims and Arabs (and Syrian refugees in particular). Presidential campaign rhetoric soared in calls to bar entry of any Muslim to our country, to round up Muslims already here, to interrogate them and patrol their neighborhoods, to carpet bomb cities held hostage by ISIS, and murder the families of suspected terrorists. Our Syrian, Arab and other Muslim partners knew what was coming next.

- "My father called and said the windows of his store were broken."
- "Our mosque was spray painted with hateful graffiti."
- "My daughter was cursed out in school."
- "Will we ever be welcome?"

Chicago

About one hundred staff at the ELCA national headquarters in Chicago met in the lobby and silently walked outside. In the midst of a field in the plaza we all fell down and stayed on the ground. Names of black men killed by police officers were read. Eric Garner, Freddie Gray, Michael Brown, and on and on....I remembered other names from previous places of ministry... Phillip Pannell, Teaneck, New Jersey...Amadou Diallo, the Bronx....Since that time we have added still more with disturbing regularity: St Paul, Baton Rouge, Montgomery, Raleigh, Baltimore...

Each new tragedy has ramped up the anger, the frustration, the seething racial uneasiness. Black colleagues tired of explaining that the "All Lives Matter" response to "Black Lives Matter" completely misses the point. Two parallel worlds—white privilege and the daily black experience of bred-in-the-bone racism—opaque to each other, with no easy place of convergence. Blacks being killed by cops on a regular basis. Now white cops being specifically targeted for execution.

We find ourselves so sharply polarized; we have so much to lament.

We stayed on the ground in silence while the names of the victims were spoken, then rose, brushed ourselves off, and walked into the cafeteria for a conversation. We heard soft-spoken African American colleagues tell about teaching their children survival tactics when stopped by the police. African American and Latino Church staff began to let out some anger, telling tales of being profiled and stopped and insulted by police. We heard stories of everyday racism in everyday encounters on buses, in stores, trains, parks, our own place of work. We listened carefully to one another. There were tentative expressions of understanding, solidarity, and reconciliation. We found ourselves in a passionate, awkward, holy space. Testimony to insidious racism came out of hiding in our national Church headquarters for a brief moment. Lamentation walled in by anger, usually cushioned by silence, leaking out.

Lisbon

For years Abrahamic Conferences between interfaith delegations from the United States and religious, political, academic and business leaders from Iran have been convened under the auspices of the International Peace Research Institute Oslo (PRIO)

The conferences have brought together religious leaders, scholars and public servants from the three Abrahamic religions from the two countries. A shared monotheism, with common roots in the patriarch Abraham, is the spiritual foundation of these proceedings. Building on this foundation, the participants have sought to achieve a better understanding of the issues that unite and separate their respective nations, cultures, and people and to consider ways of improving mutual relations. This is an effort to promote peace between two countries which do not know each other and could go to war. Religious dialogue drives this back channel for hoped-for public engagement in diplomacy leading to peace .

In the beginning we heard mostly the anger, the enduring mutual caricatures our two nations countenance about each other, distrust, and a history of mutual bad behavior. In Lisbon, where the topic was "Statecraft in the Abrahamic Traditions," the gloves came off. A shouting match erupted over the personal suffering of Iranians in the room and their families due to the sanctions, particularly the lack of access to critical medicines. Both sides erupted over Israel and Palestine. The "Great Satan" and the "Evil Empire" behaved like that toward each other. One ayatollah looked at me and said: "You western religionists are not serious. You are dilettantes, because you would allow God to be mocked." To which I shot back: "We don't understand your fatwas condemning people to death for something they said." The cacophony, anger and incomprehension of a theocracy sitting across the table from a secular society with a religious veneer, with war possible around the corner, finally began to turn to lament.

Fargo

"What happens when we feel we are losing our voice?" Pastors were asking each other that question at a retreat for rostered leaders from the Eastern North Dakota Synod. An immigrant had committed a brutal crime in Fargo. The ensuing public clamor tucked into the fear and anger attending our broken immigration system and terroristic acts of violence in our country and around the world. The pushback, spurred by internet trolls, media and anti-immigration and anti-Islam organizations, flowed into the membership of our congregations. Leaders of Lutheran Social Service agencies in North Dakota and Minnesota who serve immigrants and resettle refugees were particular targets of virulent attacks and threats to personal safety. The bishop of the synod and the Director for Lutheran Social Services in North Dakota stood before the pastors of the synod and shared their experiences. Some pastors sadly felt that they had lost their own voices in their congregations, so deep was the anger and fear expressed. They shared what some of their members were saying:

- "They are bringing jihad, part of a plot to push Sharia law and change the way of life in our community."
- "How dare we bring terrorists into our community?"
- "I can't believe our own Lutheran Church is doing this to us? I will not support a Church which does this."

Pastors struggled to help one another find the lament beneath the anger.

Jerusalem, by the Sheep Gate: An Exegesis

> Now in Jerusalem by the Sheep Gate there is a pool, called in Hebrew Bethzatha, which has five porticos. In these lay many invalids—blind, lame and paralyzed. One man was there who had been ill for thirty-eight years. When Jesus saw him lying there and he knew that he had been there a long time, he said to him, 'Do you want to be made well?' The sick man answered him, "Sir, I have no one to put me into the pool when the water is stirred up; and while I am making my way, someone else steps down ahead of me." Jesus said to him, "Stand up, take your mat, and walk."
>
> John 5:1-9

"In these lay many invalids—blind, lame, and paralyzed. One man was there who had been ill for thirty-eight years..." This is a story about tough love. As I recall the days after the September 11 attacks fifteen years ago, initially our hearts were opened. After the adrenaline rush of magnificent response to disaster, though, comes the spiritual and psychic steeling of those who settle into the new reality that follows every tragedy. Our hearts begin to close. We stare into the abyss. I saw a diminution of spiritual capital and energy in our synod in the months, and then the years after the tragedy. I believe that our society remains stuck there today. Strategies that initially got us through the night become ossified into harmful patterns of behavior. We overeat, drink too much, withdraw, make bad decisions. Fault lines become fissures. After a tragedy or crisis, congregational and personal conflicts often take on a bitter tone, call processes take longer, low-grade depression palls every meeting. Five years after 9/11, one third of our pastors were no longer serving in their calls. Some left the active ministry altogether and

> Tragedies put additional heat on things already stressed before the disaster befell. The lamentations become more shrill.

named 9/11 as the reason. Tragedies put additional heat on things already stressed before the disaster befell. The lamentations become more shrill. "Is it nothing to all you who pass by?"

I will never forget how I felt, about a year and a half after 9/11, when that event and the people in New York, Washington, D.C., and Pennsylvania disappeared from the regular prayers at the Eucharist of the Conference of Bishops meeting. The world moved on, though we remained stuck. Something hard and bitter emerges from our ground zeros. But our hearts need to be opened once more. We need to move not "on" but "out." Outside ourselves, out toward the greater pain of the world.

Once upon a time Jesus showed up at the hour of worship in Jerusalem. At that place is a pool called Bethesda and in the narthex (five of them actually) lay many invalids on their mats...blind, lame, paralyzed. It was a kind of Darwinian system of health care; those with the means, with the help, with the right connections, resources, friends, got to the pool in time to get healed. One man had lain there on his mat for thirty-eight years, in sight of the healing pool but always a day late and a dollar short.

When Jesus saw him lying there and knew that he had been there a long time, he said to him, "Do you want to be made well?" Jesus notices the man's suffering and helplessness. He *knew he had been there a long time.* There are echoes of the voice speaking to Moses from the bush: *For I have seen the affliction of my people—I know their suffering.* God has noticed the suffering in our many tragedies. God wants to be in the breach with us. How does the Church walk that hope out into the public arena?

But why did Jesus ask the question he asked? He stands before someone chronically ill, lame, and unable to walk for thirty-eight years and asks a question which seems to have the most obvious answer: *Do you want to be made well?* Why would gentle Jesus ask a cripple a question like that? It sounds insensitive, almost like a taunt. You can almost hear the man grumble to himself, "Well, what do you think, J.C.?"

But the question rouses the man to a spirited response. He was just lying there, but now he is animated, ticked. He spits out his anger: *Sir, I have no one to put me into the pool when the water is stirred up; and while I am making my way, someone else steps down ahead of me.*

Why, indeed, would Jesus ask this man that question: *Do you want to be made well?* Yet it is the only question that matters. If he doesn't, he will continue to make a life for himself sitting by the side of the pool. Our pathologies can domesticate us. Our anger and fear can paralyze us.

*Let us consider how to provoke one another to love and good works...*as we are reminded in Hebrews. "You, sisters and brothers on your mat. Do you want to be made well?" It's the only question for congregations stalled in their ministry, timid in their stewardship, lax in their discipleship, stifled in their imagination about the future, afraid of the changing communities outside their doors, hesitant to engage their own members in issues of justice, welcoming the stranger, and seeking interfaith encounters. It is the only question for those of us who have endured tragedy and resent the whole world moving on while we are stuck. "You, heart closed, turned inward, still seething, paralyzed by what happened. Do you really want to be made well? Do you want to get in the pool or not?" It's the only question for a world paralyzed by anger, sitting beside the pool on the mat of its many divisions. It is the only question for a mainline denomination like the ELCA, and its sister communions as they see a generation fall away, and lose members, resources, influence, courage and imagination. Do we really want it? Do we really want to be made well or will we clutch our rationalizations, our fears, our addictions, our self-delusions and self-absorption and talk about why we never get to the pool? Will we stop failing to drag ourselves to the pool long enough to notice the healer standing in our midst?

Jesus said to him, "Stand up, take your mat, and walk." Notice that Jesus never touches the man or puts him in the water. Even the word for "rise" in the Greek is a reflexive verb. You can't raise someone else, you can only raise yourself. The man by the pool was caught in a thirty-eight year cycle of apathy and anger. The root meaning for the Norse word "angr" is "grief." It is mourning the distance between what was...and what has become; it is grief over the distance between what is and what ought to be. Jesus found a man crippled in more ways than one...He was apathetic (*a-pathos*, without feeling). Jesus' challenge stirred the man to grieving anger. The world—and the Church—will never move past the many tragedies and crises we are asked to address in ways that heal and serve until we get in touch with our anger and shout it out in exorcising grief. We need to unleash the lamentations stuck in our throats. Creating space for that, in the name of Jesus, is the gospel mission for all of us in these latter days.

Lamentation will move our values. This kind of anger will break our hearts open again. God can work with this kind of grief. Do you want to be made well? Then stand up! Get up!

But then Jesus does something else which jars us. Once the man has stood up, he is finally free to walk after thirty-eight years, he is about to take the first step into unencumbered freedom.... *And Jesus says, "take up your mat."* Jesus makes him take up his mat. In some translations he makes the man put the mat on his back. Why? Well, healing has led to testimony. The mat became part of the man's story of God's healing providence. You have to hook your hope up with your history. Those who are healed have a story to tell. The call to healing is a call not to leave our mats behind or pretend they are not there. Moses approached the burning bush in the wilderness with a mat strapped to his back. He was a fugitive and had killed somebody. It's why God could use him. Since the unbelievable horror, flying bodies, communal terror and grief on that beautiful September day in New York in 2001, I have been dragging that mat on my back every single day.

The call to healing does not make light of the divisions amongst us, of what we have been through, of what we have lost. It is a call to walk away from apathy and also from hot anger. It is a call to cool *angr*, the grief of the gulf between what was and what has become; between what is and what should be. It is a holy longing to be well. It is a resolve to turn our gaze from the pool reflecting back our paralysis and apathy and to look into the eyes of Jesus standing with us in the breach. Jesus, the one who calls us to the place of anger transformed to healing grace for the life of the world.

The Mission Table in the World

We often speak about *the perfect table of creation*, where all creation was in harmony with the Creator.

We consider *the broken table*, and the sorrow and death of this world which has lost its perfect community and mutual relationship with the Creator.

We also remember *the kitchen table* where we heard stories of our biblical and familial ancestors, where our faith, culture, values were formed. Do you remember your kitchen table when you were growing up? What was on it? Who sat there? Do you remember the aromas? What did you talk about? It was at that family table that I discovered my deepest identity. At the kitchen table we lit the candles and sang Jesus songs in Advent, we heard the immigrant story of our grandparents. Hearing my son sing to my new grandson reminds me that those very songs were sung by my grandmother, my parents, and my wife, and me to generations of Bouman children.

We regard *the altar table of our congregations* as the table which unites the kitchen tables of our parish. Here we serve the family meal, at this table we hear stories of our ancestors, are offered the gift of faith, shared across the generations.

But mission requires that we leave the kitchen and altar tables where we have grown comfortable to form *new tables with our neighbors*: public tables of renewal, reconciled relationships, restored vision for the life of the world God loves.

Mission tables are meant to evoke the density of identity, faith, values, culture. Mission tables evoke the baptismal fonts and communion tables stretched out in public for the life of the world. This is a time when we can feel defeated, losing our imagination and even our hope. So many congregations and religious institutions are struggling to make ends meet, there has been so much crisis and pain. In 2 Kings 4:1-7 we meet a widow whose husband has died and whose children will be sold to pay her debts. In her helplessness she appeals to Elisha. "What do you want from me?" he asks, restoring her own dignity to name her pain. "What do you have in the house?"

he asks, reminding her that she is gifted. Her one jar of oil will be enough. "Leave the house," he tells her, sending her to get empty vessels from her neighbors, restoring her to communal relationships. Her one jar of oil is poured into all the empty vessels of her neighbors, the abundance of God filling her once-empty life with resources and hope. That is what we must do in mission. In our congregations we must learn to ask: "What do we have in the house?" We are gifted, God is not holding out on us. Then we must leave the house, taking our empty vessels as we enter God's mission in renewed relationships.

> We must learn to ask: "What do we have in the house?" We are gifted, God is not holding out on us.

The Gospel of Luke in Chapters 6-10 brings Matthew's Sermon on the Mount down to the plain, "the level place." The table moves closer to the people and poverty becomes literal, not just spiritualized. *Blessed are the poor in spirit.* Imagine Jesus' teaching coming alive as he speaks about the reign of God as a stone thrown in the water, rippling out in concentric circles. The stone thrown in the water is his message. *He came down with them and stood on a level place, with a great crowd of his disciples...All in the crowd were trying to touch him, for power came out from him and healed all of them. Then he looked at his disciples and said: "Blessed are you who are poor for yours is the kingdom of God."*

Jesus teaches. The stone hits the water. The ripples move outward. After preaching about mission, Jesus put legs on the sermon and lived it. *After Jesus had finished all his sayings in the hearing of the people, he entered Capernaum.* In Capernaum words become deeds. Jesus' teaching crosses boundaries and engages the most vulnerable: a centurion's servant, the widow at Nain. He attends to the lamentations he encounters. He repeats his vision for the reign of God and its mission to John's disciples: *Tell John what you have seen and heard.* He describes to them a mission of restoration and reconciliation, where the blind see, the lame walk, lepers are cleansed, the deaf hear, the dead are raised up, the poor have good news brought to them.

Jesus teaches, then acts, giving integrity to the message. Think of that story in Chapter 2 of Mark's Gospel of the hole in the roof. Jesus teaches about the forgiveness of sins, but then drives home the message by healing the paralytic. Here is what happens when the reign of God comes near, when the teachings of Jesus are enacted: a paralytic who had to be carried into the house walks out! What would that look like in our churches and their communities today?

Now see the ripples move even further outward. In Luke Chapter 8, the mission expands, leadership expands, the communal servants of the mission grow and are challenged and inspired by the accompaniment of Jesus. Jesus continues to act on his teachings, but now he intentionally takes people with him, teaching by example and preparing them for their role. Every mission leader is both apprentice and mentor: *Soon afterwards he went on through cities and villages, proclaiming and bringing the good news of the kingdom of God. The twelve were with him, as well as some women who had been cured of evil spirits and infirmities, Mary Magdalene, Joanna, and Susanna.* This is action reflecting pedagogy. Jesus engages the twelve and the three women who are wounded healers. He is showing them and taking them with him. The circles ripple further outward.

What might this action/reflection accompaniment look like in the life of a congregation? Let me share one example. Each year in the Christmas season youth groups go Christmas caroling, often to homebound members or nursing homes. The next time you go with your group to a nursing home don't send the young people home when the visit is over. Gather and reflect on the experience. Ask some questions. What did you hear? What did you smell? What were you thinking and feeling? What did you see in the faces? Let them talk about what they have just gone through. Then read the story of the Presentation of Jesus in the temple and talk about Simeon and Anna.

In Luke Chapter 9 the ripples continue to flow outward. Jesus takes the training wheels off the bicycle of mission...now you go do it... *Then Jesus called the twelve together and gave them power and authority over all demons and to cure diseases, and he sent them out to proclaim the kingdom of God and*

to heal...take nothing for your journey, no staff, bag or money or bread...what-
ever house you enter stay there, and leave from there...they departed and went
throughout the villages, bringing the good news and curing diseases everywhere.

Do you notice the stance of this communal band of missionary leaders? They travel light. They leave behind the props of their daily existence...
staff, bag, money, bread. They leave their own table and go forth into the
community as guests, vulnerable, finding themselves at the kitchen tables
of their neighbors, eating the food put in front of them. Mission is the
seeking of hospitality at the tables of our neighbors
in the world, not the other way around. We don't
approach our neighbors primarily to catalogue and
meet their needs. God is already there. Grace is all
around them. Great competence and giftedness is
already present. We go to tell our story and listen to
the stories of our new hosts around their own table.
We are seeking to be partners, communal artisans
for new space, builders of new tables. We understand that in telling stories, in invitations, in seeking and offering hospitality, all of our tables will be
renewed, transformed, repurposed. Community is
for those who cast their lots together. Community brings accountability:
needs will be met, sure, but the terms of engagement are the ethos and
vision of the mutual table.

> Mission is the
> seeking of
> hospitality at
> the tables of our
> neighbors in the
> world, not the
> other way around.

In Chapter 10, Jesus explicitly commands the visitors not to take bread
with them. Why is that? Well, what did our parents teach us about correct
behavior when a guest? "Eat what is put in front of you." We do not bring
bread because we will eat the bread of our hosts. We will be guests. We will
become "companions," those with whom we share bread. In Spanish, Latin
and French the word companion means "con" (with) "pan" (bread). And in
sharing bread we all become companions with one another and with Jesus,
the ultimate host at every table. Mission is Eucharist. Eucharist is mission.

The ripples of mission engage all of us. In Luke's Chapter 10 the fledgling mission cadre expands, the Lord appoints the seventy (that's all of us!) and sends them out in pairs to every place and town where he needs to go. *The harvest is plentiful and the laborers are few. Therefore ask the Lord of the harvest to send out laborers into his harvest.* He sends them—sends us—out two-by-two as companions seeking companions. Again he instructs: Travel light, take it to the people, into their homes and communities. Don't take bread, because you will eat your neighbors' bread.

This, then, is the pattern of mission, the church-going public. We leave the kitchen and altar tables, and seek welcome and hospitality at the tables of our neighbors.

Listening our way toward a vision for mission.
Early in my parish ministry I learned about the effectiveness of the community organizing arts in helping congregations become competent in their mission of setting tables in the world, new public space, as signs of God's new creation. Central to the organizing arts is training leaders in how to listen. I learned how "The Three Great Listenings" flow through our kitchen tables to the altar table to the tables of the neighbor, to new tables of a mission of graceful accompaniment in the world.

We listen to God, explicitly in prayer, study of scripture, liturgy, witness to the presence of God in our lives and the world around us. *The narrative of the death and resurrection of Jesus for the life of the world shapes us and the tables we set.*

We listen to the Church. God's mission has a Church. We listen for the gifts God has given us in our congregations. We listen to our ecumenical allies, to the many ministries, networks, institutions and agencies to whom we are joined in mission in an asset-based way. We set broad, gifted tables for mission. The whole Church participates in God's mission.

And we listen to our neighbors in the community. Through one-on-ones with key community leaders, the guy who sells us our morning bagel, we listen, we engage, we begin to create together new tables, new space for the many stories of our turf.

POINTS FOR REFLECTION AND DISCUSSION

1. When is anger informative and constructive? When is it destructive?
   Give some examples from your own life or that of others.

2. What is your "mat" that Jesus is calling you to take up?
   Where does your resistance come from?

3. What does, or what might, companionship look like in your congregation?

4. How do you "leave light"? Where else could you leave it if you had
   the time or the inclination?

5. What—and where—are the voices you're not listening to?
   Whose voices are they?

CHAPTER FIVE

FROM PRIVATE LITURGY
TO PUBLIC MISSION

Since many have undertaken to set down an orderly account of the
events that have been fulfilled among us, just as they were handed
on to us by those who from the beginning were eyewitnesses and
servants of the word, I too decided, after investigating everything
carefully from the very first, to write an orderly account for you,
most excellent Theophilus, so that you may know the truth
concerning the things about which you have been instructed.

Luke 1:1-4

A God Like Vinnie

As I arrived to conduct the memorial service in Queens for a fireman
named Vincent, all the streets were blocked by fire engines. The streets
were filled with uniformed firemen and police for blocks around the
church. The neighborhood was shut down tight. The members and pastor of the modest neighborhood Lutheran Church practiced an incredible
ministry of hospitality, welcoming over one thousand mourners, including
representatives of the governor's and mayor's offices. This modest parish

was suddenly in the public eye, blending the rituals of the uniformed services with the liturgy of the Church, handling press, protocol and immense crowds of distraught people. Multiply that picture by thousands. We did too many memorials in that season when so many bodies were recovered.

In his sermon, Pastor Leo Longan spoke of "a God like Vinnie." A brave, baptized child of God was remembered. He had finished his shift at Ladder 35 on the West Side on the morning of September 11 and was on his way home when the first plane hit the World Trade Center. He immediately went downtown and was buried in the act of rescue when the towers fell. There were many people at the service clearly not accustomed to being in church. The conference pastors and lay members of the congregation joined the parish pastor and me, their bishop, as we sang the liturgy on behalf of those who did not know the words or were too numb with grief to sing. But writ in that tableau is precisely the context and theological task of the Church. It is for such liturgies and ministries of encounter with this world seeking enchantment that we have been ordained and baptized. The preacher was inventing a new language of engagement in which to tell the old, old story. The preacher moved from Vinnie, who died in the act of rescuing others, to God, whose rescue of the world from sin, death and the evil one was accomplished at the cross, another life laid down for others.

Luke uses two important Greek words in the prologue to his Gospel , when he speaks of his desire to write an ordered account of the life, ministry, and teaching of Jesus.

The first word is *parédosan*, "deliver" or "to hand on," appearing in the phrase "just as they were handed on to us by those who from the beginning were eyewitnesses…" The word *paradosis* might be used to describe the passing down of a baptismal dress through generations, or the Yankee sweatshirt worn with pride and handed down from older brother to younger brother to little cousin. This word is central to Luke's concept of continuity. The *paradosis* is the handing down of the message, from Adam and Eve to Paul and Priscilla and even to today, summing up the continuity of God's salvation. The great "hand-me-down" of the Gospel moves all our waiting and searching moments into the stream of biblical faith, into the journey of all of God's faithful people. Others have lamented before us. There have been other ground zeros. Our baptism folds us into this handed-down faith and gives depth and context to our human longing for meaning. After a tragedy people will not be satisfied connecting to the thin air of wishful thinking or restored by spiritual bromides. The Gospel is the promise of God to love us unconditionally through the death and resurrection of Jesus. This *paradosis* is conveyed through the power of the Holy Spirit in the re-enchantment of Word and Sacraments. So then, the memorial liturgy for Vinnie was *paradosis*, and the thousands gathered, who may not have known the words or the story or the arcane insider language of the Church, were yet in the company and within hearing of the great "hand-me-down" of the cross and the resurrection of Jesus, the grace that is all around us.

The second word in Luke's first chapter that is relevant here is *asphaleia*, usually translated as "truth" in this verse, so: *"that you may know the truth concerning the things of which you have been instructed."* But *asphaleia* doesn't mean literal facts, evidence, or clinical proof; rather something more like *assurance, comfort,* or even *safety.* The word names what we are waiting for in faith, what the dazed survivor of tragedy seeks. *Asphaleia* is the place where the old, old story connects in one human heart. *Asphaleia* is hands grasping us in the dark of the A Train as we seek our way forward. This is the pastoral and missionary art needed today: to connect the old, old story with a public long bereft of the language of the Church. To engage the world with the "hand-me-down" of the Christian faith. To bring together *paradosis* and *asphaleia* on the A Train. This assurance and comfort is based on the great hand-me-down scriptural story, reaching back to Abraham, Sarah and Hagar, centering in the womb of Mary, exploding through the power and preaching in the Spirit in Jerusalem, Samaria, Rome, and even the grieving hearts of New York City. *Asphaleia* is the dependence of the believer, not on the events of the proximate moment, rational understanding, correct prayer, pat answers, or anything else but this: that the dying and rising Christ lives for us eternally and is with us in every waiting, lamenting, seeking moment. Romans 8, "nothing can separate us from the love of Christ," is not about coping, but about managing to find God's grace, which is always there, even—or perhaps especially—in our darkest hours.

At the eucharistic table, hard truth is declared, the world's old narrative is told, and God's promises are entertained. *Christ has died.* Vinnie has died. We say it and face it. *Christ has risen.* Vinnie has been buried with Christ by baptism into death, so that just as Christ was raised from the dead by the power of the Father, so too Vinnie will walk in newness of life. *Christ will come again.* And bring us home where Vinnie awaits, "with angels and archangels and all the company of heaven...in every time and every place."

> Romans 8, "nothing can separate us from the love of Christ," is not about coping, but about managing to find God's grace, which is always there, even—or perhaps especially—in our darkest hours.

Vinnie's funeral, then, is a parable for the mission of the Church moving forward. Thousands show up for worship not knowing the words to the liturgy or the details of the story, but bringing with them their own raw sorrow and hope. They bring childhood memories, snippets of passages like the 23rd Psalm and the Lord's Prayer memorized by heart, or the fading memory of churchgoing parents. The faithful remnant of the congregation, understanding this, gathers to sing the liturgy for them. The preacher invents a language to engage them: "A God like Vinnie." And then signs and symbols connect *asphaleia* to hearts longing for a *paradosis* that will get them through the night. They people line up, many for the first time in years, and come forward with outstretched hands. You can see it in their eyes as they approach: the hope, the doubt, the sorrow, the anger, the reverence, the faith. Bread placed in the outstretched hand connects, a tactile and incarnate assurance of God's grace.

Worship in the World; the World in Worship

> No, I have not lost my faith. The expression "to lose one's faith," as one might a purse or a ring of keys, has always seemed to me rather foolish. It must be one of those sayings of the bourgeois piety, a legacy of those wretched priests of the eighteenth century who talked so much. Faith is not a thing one "loses," we merely cease to shape our lives by it.
>
> Georges Bernanos, *Diary of a Country Priest*

It might be of some value at this point to share some liturgies in which public mission and meaningful liturgy connect in a world of conflict and poverty. This is going public "from the center," the heartbeat of Word and Sacraments and the gathered faithful. Where do you see these connections in your own worship? The connections we forge between faith and daily living drive the purpose we bring to the A Train every Monday morning.

The Public Table

> Then he said to them, "Go your way, eat the fat and drink sweet wine and send portions of them to those for whom nothing is prepared, for this day is holy to our LORD; and do not be grieved, for the joy of the LORD is your strength.
>
> Nehemiah 8:10

Our delegation approaches the village of Bushasha, Tanzania, near Lake Victoria by the border with Uganda and Rwanda. We hear the welcome before we see it. As the beating drums anticipate our arrival, as we pull up into this poor and destitute village, the crowd begins to shout, "Karibu! Karibu!" In Swahili, "welcome, and welcome again in the name of Jesus!" This is part of the world where every meal, every day is a struggle. Praying "give us this day our daily bread" is a literal prayer and what you are going to eat that day must be scratched from the stubborn, rocky soil in front of you.

Yet our hosts have prepared for us a feast. The rubble of the church lay in the background, destroyed by Idi Amin's bombs years ago. They cannot afford the bricks to restore it. Under the shade of wide acacia trees we worshipped the God of abundance and celebrated the Eucharist.

The local pastor told me that they had saved much of the food we were served for many days in order to greet us with their abundance. He also told me that his congregation used their welcome of our delegation as a means to collect the food necessary to feed the poorest among them. Word had gone out: On this day, at the church, everyone will eat. So, from a place that was apparently absent of even two loaves or any fish, God's generosity emerged. The great faith of the people produced a vision of the world as it should be when we truly hear the words of Jesus to the disciples at the feeding of the 5,000, "You give them something to eat." No one will go hungry this day. This African church believes that the one who gives the command is the one who provides the food. They understand that when God places the table of the Eucharist in the midst of the world, that it is good news for the poor.

> When God places the table of the Eucharist in the midst of the world, it is good news for the poor.

During the offertory the people rise and move toward the altar. They put money into the bags. Those too poor to have money bring what they possess. Sugarcane. A goat led by a tether. A bunch of bananas. Bolts of cloth. An egg. Cassava. Yams. Everyone brings something. Everyone bears a gift. After the liturgy, the gifts are auctioned. Those with money buy from those who have none. It all goes to the Lord. All have gifts to bring. Some of the food for the feast is also placed on the altar, a reminder that we are fed by a God of abundance.

I had the privilege of standing at the full table and celebrating the Eucharist that day. The timing was incredible. As I held up the bread and wine, consecrating these carnal elements as the body and blood of Christ, the non-Christian neighbors began to amble down the hillside for the meal. There was no artificial division between sacred and secular that day. This Eucharist was not to be a private, catered escape from the world. The world was present, invited to be in the midst of it.

There is no sacred as opposed to secular. Because God is everywhere, everything in our lives is inescapably sacred. The Eucharist cannot be trivialized to "cultic rite," "right religion," or "spiritual exercise," or even a "faith practice," as if there were some realm in existence not lived in the presence of God and imbued with the inspiration of the Holy Spirit. To celebrate the Eucharist is not to baptize life with an extraneous dousing of God. It rather recognizes the presence of the incarnate Lord in everything. The carnal vessels of water, bread and wine, eating and drinking, root the grace of God in the things of this world

Detroit House Blessing

> Bless the four corners of this house
> and be the lintel blest,
> and bless the hearth,
> and bless the board,
> and bless each place of rest....
>
> Traditional Irish Home Blessing

Cobo Hall, Detroit. 35,000 young people convene in Detroit for the 2015 ELCA Youth Gathering. The hall is filled with the sounds and activities of the custodians of our future, living into wider worlds: sharing the journey of a refugee; following a trek for potable water; understanding the difficulty of lives plagued by disabilities...scores of interactive presentations, encounters. We gather at a site where three Habitat for Humanity homes are being built. The build is a partnership between Lutheran Campus Ministries, young people at the Gathering, and Habitat for Humanity. For three days the hammering, sawing, and building noises have been a clarion call to worship. Three homes have been framed, walls raised, rooms built where people will forge new lives. Now we gather for a blessing. Think of all the actions in the world which have brought us to this moment of prayer:

- The owners of the homes, whose sweat equity in clearing the land is a firm foundation of pride and agency.
- Campus pastors, youth and their leaders.
- The capacity of Habitat for Humanity to form coalitions of hope to rebuild lives and communities.

Think as well about the public decisions that shaped this moment:

- The withdrawal of jobs, infrastructure, racial segregation, the abandonment of capital, the criminal negligence of public servants, the legacy of slavery and the appropriation of black lives, wealth and property.
- The decision of many church members to leave the beleaguered neighborhoods and replant their lives and churches elsewhere.

Yet here we are in Detroit, standing in the framed future homes with lit candles, new homeowners, builders and young Christians together. When Jimmy Carter attended an event like this in New York City years ago he said that most people think Habitat for Humanity is about the house. He said it is not. We live in a society in which a person of privilege and a person in poverty never have to be in the same room, hear the same conversation, occupy the same space. He said we live parallel lives. He said Habitat for Humanity is about new space, new relationships, transforming interactions, mutual destiny.

With lit candles, prayer and song, we move through the homes, blessing new spaces for grace. We are guests of the new owners, and all of us guests of Jesus.

We move into the kitchen. I imagine where the kitchen table will be placed, a lit candle upon it. I think about who will be around the table.

A Word about Tables

The image of a table is a useful way to understand the activity and mission of religious institutions attempting to address public life in our world in a time of conflict. In a recent book, *The Mission Table*, I describe the relationships among the tables of our lives.

A table is the central image for this book. Tables are about relationships and community. The tables of our lives center our trust in a God who offers perfect relationship. The God we call the Holy Trinity and in whom we have been baptized is perfect love and community. The fullness of this God is pleased to dwell in this world in the life, death, and resurrection of Jesus. What shapes the tables of our communities of Jesus, each baptized disciple, and his or her mission in the world is the biblical drama of the story of Israel; the paschal mystery of the life, mission, death, and resurrection of Jesus; and the New Testament Church that emerged from these narratives.

- Our tables are expressions, in the name of Jesus, of God's love and community:
- The perfect table of creation, where all creation was in harmony with the Creator.
- The broken table and the sorrow and death of this world, which has lost its perfect community and mutual relationship with the Creator.
- The kitchen table where we heard stories of our biblical and familial ancestors, where our faith, culture, and values were formed.
- The altar table of our congregations, which unites the kitchen tables of our parishes.
- New tables that we form with our neighbors: tables of renewal, reconciled relationships, and restored vision for the life of the world God loves.

We form these public tables with our neighbors of all denominations and faiths. They take shape when kitchen and altar tables merge with new and renewed tables in the community—both locally and globally—where new relationships of mutuality and reconciliation are formed for the life of the world.

A Word about Sacraments

Consider this new table in a suburb of New Jersey. In a "listening in the community" process of mission discernment in which our congregation and conference were engaged, homeless women and children emerged as a high priority. After baptizing a homeless child and his mother we could not resist the missional power of the sacraments. We bought the house next door to the church and began planning transitional housing for homeless women and children. There was much resistance from the community, and some from the congregation itself, but the leadership resolved to see this through. The Sunday before the first mother and her two children would begin to live in the house next door we entered into the evangelical power of the eucharistic table. After the communion liturgy, but before the benediction, our entire congregation processed to the house next door. We went from the Lord's table out into the street. The crucifer, acolytes, book bearer and children carrying bread and wine from the altar led the family of Jesus into the house next door. We placed the bread and wine on the kitchen table. We imagined a mother and her young children around the table. In the kitchen we prayed for the mother and her babies, and for this sacred kitchen table, and offered a prayer of thanks that we were privileged along with our new neighbors to be guests of Jesus in this world. We then reassembled in the church for the benediction. "Go in peace, serve the Lord," echoed into our ears as we left for our own kitchen tables to continue the Eucharist. The world is at the altar table, and the altar table is at all of the tables of our world.

Groundbreaking in Juba

We gather for a groundbreaking liturgy on a barren plot of ground in the Referendum neighborhood of Juba, the beleaguered capital city of the new nation of South Sudan in Africa. This will be the site of the first Lutheran church, clinic and community center in the fragile nation ripped apart by civil war, ethnic brutality, and massive internal migration. This neighborhood had been the site of an ethnic massacre during the civil war. Now it is home to many internally displaced refugees of both Dinka and Nuer tribes, who had been combatants in the war. The ground is barren and rocky, surrounded by the shell of a wall. Stakes marked with strips of white cloth are pounded into the ground, delineating where the center's foundation will be. The world in the liturgy. The liturgy in the midst of the world.

A tall young man sweltering in a business suit and tie in the 105 degree heat stood with his fiancée during the liturgy. The day before our delegation had walked around the neighborhood and noticed a large open space across the road from the space where we would be breaking ground. Conversations with neighbors eventually led us to the owner, Mathiang, who came out to meet us. When he asked why we were inquiring about his property, we shared our vision for a church, community center, health facilities—spaces for grace, healing and reconciliation. He shared our excitement about the vision. He invited our delegation to meet for lunch at his fiancée's restaurant. Conversations continued throughout the day and evening. His father, a very influential Member of Parliament, had given the property to Mathiang, who had studied at a college in Minnesota and had worshipped at a Lutheran church in Fargo, North Dakota. After confirming that we were serious, and that we could deliver what we promised, Mathiang offered us the additional land. Our conversations were deep, and spiritual. After the liturgy he took us to the Parliament building to meet and pray with his father who, after kicking our tires (architect plans, budgets, etc.), gave his blessing to his son's plan to deed the property to our new mission. He and his son expressed broken hearts at the suffering of their people, anger at the forces which caused it and were enriched by it, and amazed that our paths crossed and they had a way to give back both to the country they love and the God they worship. In all of this our vision was growing, expanding. I guess you would have to say that the Holy Spirit convened the world which entered our groundbreaking liturgy.

Many neighbors wandered into the liturgy, some curious, some hopeful, some amazed that people from around the world were walking among them. The liturgy was public, in the midst of the world, and the world was present. The hem of the garment of Jesus was visible, touchable. Think of the table movement here in the worship of the Church: so many kitchen tables, altar tables, tables assembled to give birth to a new table of God's grace. The rituals, prayers, reading of scripture, shovel breaking through the dirt—the *paradosis*—were a sign of comfort—*asphaleia*—as dirt and stones were moved away, and we imagined a new space for grace on a hot day in Juba.

1. In what ways has God shown up in your life that you have found surprising? Where have you encountered "Vinnies," and what about them has encouraged, informed, or confounded you?

2. How does our language need to change in order to better engage with the world? Be specific.

3. How does your congregation "set the table?" Is it as intentionally inclusive as it could be?

4. Where should tables be set that aren't being set now?

CHAPTER SIX

THE PUBLIC MISSION TABLE

The city needs a soul, and the people must give it.
Pope John Paul II, Yankee Stadium, 1978

Then they said, "Let us start the building!" So they committed
themselves to the common good...Next to them Uzziel son of
Harhaiah, one of the goldsmiths made repairs. Next to them
Hananiah, one of the perfumers, made repairs; and they
restored Jerusalem as far as the Broad Wall...above the Horse
Gate, the priests made repairs, each one opposite his own
house...

Nehemiah 2:18; 3:8; 3:28

All politics is local.

Senator Tip O'Neill

Rebuilding

When Nehemiah urged the returning exiles, and those who had been living in captivity in Jerusalem, to rebuild the walls of the city, their approach took a page from community organizing. Each rebuilt the part of the wall nearest their homes and businesses. Chapter 3 of Nehemiah names the clans, the artisans and guilds, the businesses who together rebuilt the walls of the city nearest to them and thereby most in their self-interest. They re-established themselves in the city by hunkering down by their own section of the wall and making it new again. Individually, each group had a piece of the wall. Each claimed their turf. But communally, brick by brick, the repaired sections added up to more than themselves. Together they were rebuilding a city. Together they were rebuilding their faith. Together they were renovating their covenant with God. Individually they were guilds and clans and businesses and families, but communally they were rebuilding their solidarity as a people.

When all were gathered together at the Water Gate after rebuilding their homes and settling in their towns and neighborhoods, Ezra read from the Scriptures, and the people wept to hear God's word again. They gave their Amens! and worshipped God. They celebrated with joy, eating and drinking and sharing their food with those who did not have any. We learn in Chapter 8 that the leaders took great care that people understood the readings.

> **So they read from the book, from the law of God, with interpretation. They gave the sense, so the people understood the reading...and all the people went their way to eat and drink and to send portions and to make great rejoicing, because they had understood the words that were declared to them.**
>
> **Nehemiah 8:8, 12**

With understanding and interpretation the people were able to get the big picture. They were able to grasp again their destiny as a people, that the forgiveness and reconciliation with their God and one another was one and the same. Life was about more than survival. Life had meaning. As they went back to their homes and occupations by their section of the repaired wall they were again able to see the Day Approaching.

The Day Approaching

> Let us hold fast to the confession of our hope without wavering.
> For the one who promised is faithful. And let us consider how
> to provoke one another to love and good works, not neglecting
> to meet together as is the habit of some. But encouraging one
> another. And all the more as we see the Day approaching.
>
> Hebrews 10:22-24

The rebuilding of Jerusalem, of course, shows the rhythm of worship in the midst of the world, and the world in the midst of worship. As congregations re-root their lives into the lives of their communities, they are rebuilding their part of the wall. It is important to remember that if anyone is not equipped to rebuild their part, the whole is weaker. The community is vulnerable to the extent that any one member is vulnerable.

The Church sets and seeks hospitality at tables in the community, combining the lamentations, anger, fear, paralysis, poverty, and hunger they find there with the hope and giftedness of the world around them. The Day Approaching draws us forward and outward, toward the reconciliation, restoration, renewal which the death and resurrection of Jesus promises all creation. We will remember that it was this Jesus who sent out two-by-two, then seventy (all of us), to tables in the world as companions. That vision, and the one who sent us out to tables in the world, is our true north, our morning star.

In this chapter we will examine some of the ways in which the Church goes public in its response to the pain and vulnerability of this world. We will want to pay attention to what happens when these responses remain only at our part of the wall and fail to see the rebuilding of the whole city or of the Day Approaching. Our social ministries and ways of encountering the public can become guild worlds reduced to just meeting temporary needs instead of being an integral part of a larger vision of reconciliation and restoration. This chapter is about the re-enchantment of the

Church's public witness and service.

Can we move from programmatic and disembodied activism to a communal embrace of the world as the Body of Christ? I remember when one congregation had to rewrite a script in the New Jersey Synod. The script for the synod assembly video highlighting the ministry of a nearby urban congregation had begun something like this: "The Food Pantry and Shelter is known citywide for its programs of compassion and social service." Even though that was a true statement, the pastor told them the script got it all wrong. "We are not the Food Pantry and Shelter," he insisted. "We are a church. The pantry and shelter is one of the ways we act on the faith we share as the people of God gathered by and around Word and Sacraments. It is part of being the Body of Christ in the world." They changed the script. It now went something like this: "The family of believers at First Lutheran Church is known citywide for its ministry of compassion. One such dimension of the congregation's ministry is the Food Pantry and Shelter." They finally got the script right. Our identity as a Church in social ministry does not start with this or that program or human effort. This is the starting place and script for all ministry.

There is only one ministry. The institutional Church and individual churches must be themselves. There is no such thing as separate "social ministry," or "advocacy," or "community organizing," that is, some specialized activity that is somehow different from all else we do, pray, are.

All ministries of mercy in our congregations and institutions and denominations have their genesis in Word and Sacraments. They are part of the ministry of Christians gathering together a community of believers around these means of grace and relating them to and through Christ to one another and the world God loves. All other

> There is no such thing as separate "social ministry," or "advocacy," or "community organizing," that is, some specialized activity that is somehow different from all else we do, pray, are.

goals, vital though they may be—social justice, economic growth, power for the powerless, partnerships for social change, ideas of liberation, neighborhood renewal, immigration reform, racial justice—are derived from the self-understanding of a community gathered by and for the Word and Sacraments, always connected to the death and resurrection of Jesus in anticipation of the Day Approaching.

Biblical and Theological Foundations for Public Engagement

When asked to present a paper on Lutheran and Protestant perspectives on the topic "Statecraft in the Abrahamic Religions" for the interfaith dialogues with Iran I found a new clarity about my own tradition. What follows are some of the key biblical and theological streams which flow into Lutheran and mainline Protestant understandings of the relationship between theology and public life. These are the hunches we take with us on the A Train.

Incarnation. "A Christian ought to pray with the Bible in one hand and the New York Times in the other." This aphorism emphasizes the fact that the Western Catholic tradition, from which Lutheran and Protestant traditions flow is about the revelation of God within history. The Biblical narrative places God's activity at the center of human history. Incarnation means that the real God takes real flesh (humanity) in the real world among real people. The central historical narrative for Christian traditions is the life, death and resurrection of Jesus of Nazareth, son of God. We enter the public arena because the public square is God's and God continues to be present in the world. Public mission is discerning what God is doing in the world and setting or joining a table there.

Tzedik. Biblical tradition places the theology of the Jewish faith and communities, and then of the Christian faith and communities, within a larger socio-political and religious context. Two Hebrew words can help us here. One is *"mishpat,"* which has been translated as justice. *"Mishpat"* is the activity, the defining decisions made by those in power. The other Hebrew word is *"tzedik,"* which is best translated as righteousness. *"Tzedik"* is the communal consensus, the meta-narrative of the community, its highest ideals. The *"mishpat"* must be derived from the *"tzedik."*

Norman Gottwald, in his book *The Tribes of Yahweh* speaks of two competing narratives *(tzedik)*, or ways of understanding and being in the world. One was the ethos of survival coming out of the Canaanite myths and the other was the ethos of Yahweh, the God of the widows and orphans. The *mishpat* of Baal, the Canaanite God, is about power and armies and treaties. The highest good is survival. It is a public consensus about accepting coercion in an age of scarcity. The ethos of God, the creator, is a consensus of abundance and grace. I believe that the choice is still before us today in our polarized world. Baal or God?

These competing myths of scarcity and abundance are with us today. This biblical ethos of compassion for the least, the last, the most vulnerable informs political participation by many Christians today, including the Western Catholic tradition, Lutherans and many other Protestant traditions. With the *tzedik* of abundance we move to the *mishpat*, the justice for the most vulnerable. God takes sides.

Two-handed God. Lutherans believe in a two-handed God. Martin Luther was an Augustinian monk and Lutheran thinking about public faith lies ever in the shadow of St. Augustine. The Augustinian distinction between the City of God and the City of Man is expressed by Martin Luther in his doctrine of the Two Kingdoms, The kingdom of the right hand (salvation) and the kingdom of the left hand (public engagement in the world). It is out of these traditions that we get the idea of the separation of church and state. This means that our efforts to participate in public political life, to stand with the poor, to transform systems of dominance and corruption, to engage in corporate and individual acts of mercy, and to influence legislation on behalf of the most vulnerable, are not messianic. We do not claim to be ushering in the Kingdom of God by our political activity in the world. Many of today's political and liberation theologies are flawed by identifying such efforts with the absolute will of God. All activity of the kingdom of the left hand comes under judgment. It is provisional, at best a sign of the reign of God to come. That ability to live in ambiguity, guided by the *tzedik* of grace and abundance, also leaves us free to work with other men and women of good will in the public arena. Lutherans would say that the death and resurrection of Jesus (right hand) makes us free to love and serve our neighbor (left hand).

Presence. Luther, as a good Catholic, believed that *"finitum capax infinitum."* The finite is capable of the infinite. Life is sacramental. The water of baptism conveys the eternal grace of God's love. Ordinary bread and wine hold the eternal and holy presence of the body and blood of Christ. So also each Christian, each act of mercy can be a sign of God's presence. How does one know the messiah is present? The blind will see, the prisoners will be set free, there will be good news for the poor, the oppressed will go free. (See Luke 4: 16-22.) When Christians advocate for this in the political and public arena these are glimpses of the presence of the messiah, signs of shalom.

Vocation. Luther's idea of vocation is very important here. The mediating institutions of family, congregation, and neighborhood gain importance as we venture into the public arena. Christian political activity tends to want to strengthen these bonds of family, congregation, neighborhood and mutual help in the kingdom of the left hand. This is a particular strength of faith based community organizing. The life of a Christian congregation invites people into the family of believers, where by the love of God nobodies become somebodies, pain is borne, hope is sustained, and every believer is a "little Christ" to her neighbor. My vocation to follow Jesus includes my various roles as father, worker, and citizen.

Exile. The prophet Jeremiah gives a glimpse of the two kingdoms, a modest biblical realism concerning the political activity of the faith community. Israel is in exile in Babylon. They face an identity crisis. In the words of one psalm they ask "how can we sing the Lord's song in a strange land?" While never allowing them to forget Jerusalem, Jeremiah yet gives this advice: While in Babylon plant your trees, have your babies, live your daily lives fully and "seek the welfare of the city in which God has placed you in exile, pray for it, for in its welfare you will find your own." This is really important. It tells us that our mission field is here and now, in this place where God has placed us. It means building our part of the wall, keeping in our sight the rebuilding of the whole city.

Creation. Creation (the first article of the Apostle's Creed, "I believe in God the Father almighty, creator of heaven and earth") is another key to the participation of the believer in public life. In Genesis Adam and Eve were created "in the image of God." This means that they were partners with God in unfolding creation. God told them—us—to name, bless, have a hand, be involved in the organization of the created world. We were created to be stewards—subjects, not objects, of history. We were created, in the image of God, to be actresses and actors in the human drama. To have no say in your life, no way of participating in communal decisions and well-being is to be spiritually dead. We were created to participate in creation. That means that our public presence will always be seeking voices not heard, power where there is none, seats at the table for those who have been shut out.

Abundance. In America we have "red" and "blue" state ways of lining up on certain issues. We need a religious vision big enough to transcend both of these smaller visions. In all of the Abrahamic faiths there are some very clear central values. God is a God of abundance, not scarcity. God is not holding out on us. God calls us to welcome the stranger. The heart of God goes out to the poor and hungry. Orphans and widows have a special place in our scripture narratives. God is the author of Salaam, Shalom, Peace. For Christians in America issues like immigration, poverty, and hunger have very clear biblical mandates around which red and blue state folks ought to find ways to unite.

A Word about Class and Culture

During the last several presidential elections the pundits have said issues of public morality or religious values played a large role. In 2016, those polarizing issues have also included immigration, sexual identity, reproductive health, responding to gun violence and other fundamentally divisive issues. These issues describe a country divided: blue and red versions of religious values or public morality. In the midst of ongoing conversation around public morality and religious values, let us remember the role that class plays.

John is a blue collar guy from the parish I served in New Jersey. That part of New Jersey would be a red-state kind of place. Countless jobs have been lost in this industrial area. Their mayor was the most conservative of the five candidates running for the republican nomination for governor of the Garden State (an election won by Chris Christie). When I introduced a chalice for use at the Eucharist John accused me of trying to make the congregation too "Catholic." His attitudes may be described as racist, classist, and homophobic. We clashed on everything in those first years. But this was also a congregation which started a school for the children of its community, met with mayors and governors concerning affordable housing, bought the parish house next door to house homeless women and children. It was a congregation where the poor and homeless knew they were welcome. And John was in the midst of it. His conversion came when he helped plan and serve a meal for the homeless in our church basement. John sat across the table from children of God who were hungry. He listened to one story after another. He connected in a radical way, with his faith and his vocation. Because he knew and believed the Gospel he was able to act on it when given a chance. His attitudes softened.

My point is that when you meet John and the millions like him you realize that the so-called red and blue divide is not easily overcome. There is a cultural divide, one that has been there for years. What we are seeing in the polarized public arena today is smugness, contempt and ridicule fueling the class and cultural divide. Contempt for John and his version of Christianity is deep and naked among many Christians. And this divide has been there for years. The ministry of "advocacy" has, in the past, sometimes come across as smug and patronizing to John and many other faithful Church leaders I have known. And John and others have come across as judgmental, culturally naïve, even heartless. The answer to the struggle for the soul of being Christian in America, however, will never be answered by class contempt or self-righteous posturing. We can't fight two wars. We can't fight a culture war and a war on poverty. And we can't spend our time and energy vying for the upper hand in whose version of a "Christian America" will prevail. As a listening Church we must listen internally for what is on the minds and hearts of our own membership on both sides of the divide. Otherwise we have nothing to offer when we go public. And our world needs artisans of new tables where two worldviews so often opaque to each other can reconcile. Jeremiah shows us the way.

> As a listening Church we must listen internally for what is on the minds and hearts of our own membership on both sides of the divide.

An Exegesis of Jeremiah 28

> Then the prophet Jeremiah replied to the prophet Hananiah before the priests and all the people who were standing in the house of the LORD. He said, "Amen! May the LORD do so! May the LORD fulfill the words you have prophesied by bringing the articles of the LORD's house and all the exiles back to this place from Babylon. Nevertheless, listen to what I have to say in your hearing and in the hearing of all the people: From early times the prophets who preceded you and me have prophesied war, disaster and plague

against many countries and great kingdoms. But the prophet who prophesies peace will be recognized as one truly sent by the LORD only if his prediction comes true.

Then the prophet Hananiah took the yoke off the neck of the prophet Jeremiah and broke it, and he said before all the people, "This is what the LORD says: 'In the same way I will break the yoke of Nebuchadnezzar king of Babylon off the neck of all the nations within two years.'" At this, the prophet Jeremiah went on his way.

After the prophet Hananiah had broken the yoke off the neck of the prophet Jeremiah, the word of the LORD came to Jeremiah: "Go and tell Hananiah, 'This is what the LORD says: You have broken a wooden yoke, but in its place you will get a yoke of iron. This is what the LORD Almighty, the God of Israel, says: I will put an iron yoke on the necks of all these nations to make them serve Nebuchadnezzar king of Babylon, and they will serve him....'"

Then the prophet Jeremiah said to Hananiah the prophet, "Listen, Hananiah! The LORD has not sent you, yet you have persuaded this nation to trust in lies."

Jeremiah 28:5-15

A Call to Speak Clearly

Meet Jeremiah, practicing public theology at its most intense. Jeremiah thanks the prophet Hananiah for his pronouncement of impending peace and the end of exile in Babylon. "Amen!" to that vision says Jeremiah. He notes that prophets before them have prophesied war, famine, pestilence against many countries. They certainly can use a good word about peace. And Jeremiah ends this section by saying that when the word of the prophet about peace comes true, then we will know that the Lord has truly sent a prophet.

Here's the issue for Jeremiah, however: Israel has lost its way. "They have made offerings to other Gods and worshipped the works of their own hands." Therefore, the prophet says, Israel will be purified and chastened.

They will be conquered by Babylon and taken into exile until they again reclaim their vocation, not as one thug, narcissistic nation among many, living by the *tzedik* survival ethic of Baal, but as a "light to the Gentiles, a blessing to all people." They had forgotten that the God of Israel is the God of the migrant worker, the widow, the orphan, the captive, the poor; they are supposed to be a servant people. And God sent Jeremiah to warn the people that any peace short of the peace of Jahweh, any vocation short of the call to be a light to the Gentiles, is a false peace, a false vocation. Equating public morality and religious values with the prospering of the nation as a power seeking its own ends is, for Jeremiah, a moral disaster. And so he had the unpopular task of speaking clearly the word of God. No justice, no peace. And God knew that it would not be easy.

> **Gird up your loins, stand up and tell them everything I command. Do not back down before them or I will break you before them.**

> **The prophets are prophesying lies in my name...I did not send them...a lying vision who say "sword" and "famine" shall not come to this land.**

This is tough stuff to hear and Jeremiah was considered unpatriotic. He refused to conflate the religious vision with the secular vision for the nation. He refused to give a message of false peace. And yet he yearned for the true peace of God as much as any of them. God did not call Jeremiah to be the house theologian of a corrupt nation. He was called to speak clearly, with integrity, the word of the Lord and the vision of the God of the orphans and widows and victims of injustice. That vision of true peace will have its own power.

Israel did go into exile. The holy things of Jerusalem were in captivity. "How can we sing the Lord's song in a strange land?" And we recalled earlier in this chapter what happened when Israel returned to Jerusalem after the exile and rebuilt the walls of the city, and their covenant with God.

Hananiah broke the yoke and predicted victory. He died within the year and is largely forgotten. Yet the vision of peace prevails.

Our choice today is still between Baal or God; abundance or scarcity; fear and anger, or grace. With the vision of the Day Approaching clear before us, we take the A Train into the public arena. Following are some of the ways the Church can go public, and still bring people like John along with us. In fact, people like John often lead the Church out of the building and into the world.

Hunger and Poverty

The ELCA World Hunger Program has a vision that working to end hunger and poverty is essential to being the Church and being a disciple. It's in the DNA of the Church, not just a signature program. One implication of this is that we aspire to become a Church "of the poor," not "of clients," or of "objects of charity," but of sisters and brothers at the table together. Whether people in poverty, immigrants, refugees, migrants, "they are us." Another implication is that the Church will move more deeply into addressing root causes of hunger and poverty. This is incorporated into everything we do. It means a bottom line commitment to sustainable change addressing poverty, with a commitment to accompany those burdened by poverty to participate in that change (organizing and development); and to equip those who do have resources to also participate in social change (education, advocacy, listening in the community). People in poverty, people of means and privilege: we can only rise up as one Church together. ELCA World Hunger has a commitment to addressing root causes of poverty through a comprehensive approach linking and aligning all the various ways that the Church accompanies public society with the Gospel. And to do this as the Body of Christ in the world.

Around Thanksgiving every year, and other times during the year, congregations collect food for the local food pantries. Often this food is put on the altar. Sometimes our congregations participate in an "offering of letters" for advocacy ministries addressing hunger and poverty, such as our denominational advocacy offices or groups like Bread for the World. Sometimes congregations participate in community gardens or food distribution through food pantries or soup kitchens. Sometimes we make cash donations to groups such as "Feed My Starving Children" or "World Vision International," which feed the hungry and give us a direct and tangible connection with them. 95% of all congregations in the ELCA, according to the annual parochial reports, are involved in some kind of hunger ministry, most of them in the "individual acts of mercy" response like a donation of food or money to groups which feed the hungry globally and locally. I believe that we should celebrate this almost unanimous participation in direct relief and from there create a movement.

Yes, we celebrate when God's starving children are given something to eat. We joyfully participate in that ministry. But can we not also aspire to be in the starving child's world, to change it, so that her world no longer keeps her hungry and poor. So, how can the Church grow cans of corn into a movement of social justice and sustainable development? We begin where we are: donating to food banks, helping community gardens, distributing food and engaging in other relief activities. One strategy is for regional and national Church leaders to help build networks of effective approaches to ending hunger. Every congregation can listen, participate in one-on-ones with both the leaders who help alleviate poverty and those who are hungry.

The can of corn on the altar extends the altar. It mingles with the bread and wine and those who approach with outstretched hands.

Every food pantry, every shared meal, every community garden, can be a listening post. The grassroots lived experience of people in poverty will reveal stories of real lives, real aspirations, real lamentations, real giftedness, and begin to paint a picture of systemic injustice. Such a strategy could leverage networks, conversations, new emerging tables of people of privilege and people in poverty. The can of corn on the altar extends the altar. It mingles with the bread and wine and those who approach with outstretched hands.

Feeding the hungry also connects us to advocacy and education around issues related to food security, hunger and poverty. Advocacy can mean to speak on behalf of someone, like the narrator lifting up the lamentations of the Daughter of Zion. But it also means bringing to the table the actual voices themselves. That is why advocacy has to be connected to local congregations, to social service agencies that provide direct services, and also to efforts at grassroots mobilization to empower people who are customarily excluded from the table where decisions are made. Community organization amplifies the voices of those who are poor, left out, on the margins of our society.

Another way to frame this conversation is to say that privilege allows certain people to be at important tables. Through advocacy, we turn our privilege around—using it to ensure that other' voices are heard at those tables. Community organizing creates new tables with new centers of power.

So the ministry of advocacy, for instance, can make sure that programs such as SNAP which provides food for people in poverty, are included in social services budgets. Thousands are fed, or go hungry, depending upon the effectiveness of the ministry of advocacy. And that ministry is strengthened by the inclusion of voices from the grassroots who are directly affected by these decisions. Advocacy and community organizing should be integrated strategies. When they are not, then advocacy merely speaks for others who remain objects, not subjects of their history. Congregations must take their rightful place at the heart of the intersection between grassroots mobilization and advocacy.

I was blessed early in my ministry as a parish pastor in New York City to be involved in the faith based community organizing for grassroots mobilization. I have witnessed nothing since which has so effectively trained leaders, formed my own leadership habits, or enabled congregations to participate actively and effectively in the movement for justice and social change. When congregations fight for the soul of their communities and give public witness that their values and beliefs are worth fighting for they are performing an act of evangelism. People want to know more about a relevant Church, willing to engage public leaders in conversations about a shared vision for our communities, and willing to battle with them if necessary.

Fake It, Anthony!

> When faith leads to action in outward affairs, that which takes place is spiritual in the midst of the carnal. Everything our bodies do, the external and the carnal, is called spiritual behavior, if God's word is added to it and it is done in faith.
>
> Martin Luther

The annual Christmas program of the nursery school of my former parish in New Jersey is always a grand production. The students file on stage and stand on pieces of tape marking each one's spot. Behind each piece of tape is a rhythm instrument. At a certain time in the song the children are instructed to turn around, pick up the instruments and bang away with the piano.

Showtime! The children strut onto the stage and onto the tape. They sing their lungs out. Then they turn around on cue and grasp their instruments and flail away with abandon. Except on one occasion, there is a problem: the little girl next to Anthony has taken both her castanets and Anthony's tambourine. She is whaling away in rhythm heaven. Anthony comes up empty-handed and his face registers pure panic. He looks behind him again. Nothing! His face screws up as if to cry.

If we are going to talk about the Church going public in the midst of the paralysis of anger and fear and sense of dislocation which envelopes us after public tragedies or natural disasters, then the look on Anthony's face tells us all we need to know. That moment of panic, fear, abandonment plays itself out in myriad ways over moments and lifetimes. His face was mine at Ground Zero, completely cut off from any integration with faith or what I thought that I knew about the world. His was a face abandoned and ready to cry.

He sees the girl next to him shaking her castanets and his tambourine. He reaches for it and she pulls away. He strikes out at her and she pulls away, working rhythm overtime as if taunting him. He pulls his hand back again. He's going to deck her.

"Anthony!" His teacher's voice is urgent but gentle. His face begins to rearrange itself and registers recognition. The calling of his name by a familiar, trusted voice brings him back to himself.

"Anthony! Fake it!"

He smiles, relieved and secure. He does a Milli Vanilli and shakes his hands and body to the music without a tambourine, as if his instrument was in his hand. With one word from a servant of the Church, the community of Jesus kept company with a frightened child.

This moment of simple grace reveals much concerning social ministry, accompanying civil society with the Gospel, setting and joining public tables in the world. Anthony's need was satisfied because of a relationship. In all ministry relationship matters most. Too often what passes for social ministry or social service is performed by strangers who hold the poor in contempt, giving charity which is resented by the stranger receiving it.

How different the encounter of Jesus with the woman who had been bleeding for twelve years, who touched the hem of his garment in a story told in the Gospels of both Mark and Luke.

Jesus turned, *seeing* her. Not a budget line item; not the needy client with the resourced professional; not a cause. Just *her* in all her beautifully complex humanity.

And he calls her "daughter." Relationships are reordered. She is kin. Together they are building a new table where each of them belong. And he said: "Your faith has made you well." He sees and honors her giftedness.

In the Church love flows out from those willing to share their lives and their community with the stranger, but love also flows back into the Church through the giftedness and strength of those we encounter. Anthony's relationship with his teacher was enabled by the congregation's willingness to fashion a sturdy institution that would join children and their families to the competence, compassion and outreach of the parish community. And in a bottom-line age in which we think we can fix everyone's wagon and throw money at every problem, this boy's lack of an instrument was not remediated, but his need was addressed by a love willing to stand with him in the midst of his confusion and vulnerability and anger.

The Church is forever organizing itself to address human need and extend human community within the household of faith and into the world beyond. From Stephen and his six fellow deacons in the Acts of the Apostles to their successors today, faithful social ministry is not something tacked onto the Church's agenda, a sideline for some but not required of all. Compassionate action is central to the Gospel and to the one ministry of communities gathered around and by both Word and Sacraments. So let's change the name of what we may have called the "social ministry" committee to—the "Public Mission Table." It can become the means for our congregations to be voices calling out to all the world's Anthonys in the Name of Jesus.

> We need to abandon forever the notion that action in the communities that surround us is somehow peripheral to our core mission.

We need to abandon forever the notion that action in the communities that surround us is somehow peripheral to our core mission. In fact, we should see our newly dubbed Public Mission Table first and foremost as a means of evangelism. Social Ministry and evangelism must be one thing. A relevant church, engaged in the struggles of its community with its neighbors, contributing to a vision for its well-being, is a community to which people will be drawn. It is important to remember that our invitations to join us are never a requirement. True Gospel invitations are always sensitive to the history of their neighbors, some of whom have been harmed and judged by faith communities or could feel intimidated by a too strong invitation. But each program of social service or social change must include a credible invitation to participate in the fuller life of the parish.

The Public Mission Table in Practice

Putting the notion of our Public Mission Table into practice is something that any congregation can achieve with a proper understanding of purpose and by following a few practical guidelines for success.

**The Public Mission Table should attend
to the needs of those within the household of faith.**

I truly learned most powerfully about the healing power of the community of the Church when I myself received a diagnosis of cancer.

"I'll pray for you" was no longer a pious bromide, but a gift of sustaining power. All the prayers kept me in the hands of my Creator and brought to me the peace of the Healer. So many times I had said "I'll pray for you," with a kind of Protestant work ethic. Never again. Those are now holy words to me. To pray for someone is to participate in creation. The people we pray for appear before us in all their particularity and originality. Prayer shrinks the distance between the one who prays and the one in the heart of the prayer, mirroring the ministry of Jesus, whose cross and resurrection closes the distance between God and you and me.

Lying on a gurney in the hallway outside a door that warns, "Keep Out," waiting for the surgery, I was filled with anxiety. Then my wife came over with these words of comfort: "Stephen, Pastor's here." Pastor's here. My pastor stood over me, not just a nice guy, but a designated representative of the community of Jesus, a reference point to God's promises, a reminder that I am not the first one to ever have to trust God into the unknown. We prayed the Lord's Prayer together. He blessed me, tracing the sign of the cross on my forehead. Re-enchantment as they pushed me through the doors. Later, during a time of depression while at home recovering, I received a visit in New York from my dear friend from Ohio, Bishop Marcus Miller. When he showed up with bread and wine at my home I began to move from the cave into the sunlight. We are only healed into community. "Pastor's here." And such pastoral visits can be offered by the laity as well. "Pastor's here" is a communal ministry and blessing.

When I was brought home to recover, hot meals began appearing at our front door. Without any fuss the members of our congregation fed us every day for two weeks. We were connected to hope and to community by these elemental acts of kindness. The title of my favorite Raymond Carver short story is "A Small, Good Thing." The title refers to freshly baked bread and, indeed, the small good thing of food at our doorstep was manna on our road to healing.

I'll pray for you. Pastor's here. Soup's on. I learned to trust the power of these small, good things. Prayer, pastoral presence, small acts of kindness became the foundation of disaster response, whose power in a time of seeming powerlessness were already known to me in a deep and abiding way.

This means taking responsibility for the great public and political sacramental acts of the Church. When we baptize we do not leave those baptized at the font. We follow them to their school, where it matters greatly to us if they are safe and can learn. We care whether they will abuse substances, whether they will have a shot at a good job and decent housing, whether they will be formed in their baptismal faith as fellow Christians living the Gospel in the world.

**The Public Mission Table should manage ministries
of social service and corporal works of mercy.**

In one congregation I served this meant the joining of the parish—and ultimately our ELCA mission cluster of congregations—to a county-wide Inter-Religious Fellowship for the Homeless. Our social ministry committee organized our participation in IRF, which included the staffing of local shelters, administration of transitional housing, dinners for the homeless, and advocacy efforts. When we purchased the house next to our church and used it to shelter homeless families in a transitional housing program, this committee helped administer efforts to help the family get back on its feet, including getting medical help for the children, assisting job searches and looking for suitable permanent housing. The committee members also provided invitations and access into the life of the parish, including our parish nursery school, summer programs, Sunday school, and Spanish-language outreach. Finally, the social ministry committee provided training and encouragement for caregivers in these programs.

The Public Mission Table should oversee a parish-based community organizing effort.

Community organizing is the discipline that helps a parish, family, or neighborhood develop the power to sit at the table where decisions are made that shape their communal life. These grassroots organizing efforts can be found all across the country: in Appalachia; on farms; in suburban and inner-city neighborhoods.

The accomplishments of these organizations are many and varied: Nehemiah homes in Brooklyn; renewal of neighborhoods; improvement of public education; victories in the war on drugs; affordable housing; influence on local, state and national policy. But just as important have been the modest victories with which I am most familiar: saving a building on the 92nd Street in Jackson Heights in Queens; breaking ground for twelve units of affordable housing in Bogota, New Jersey; the formation of a charter school in the south Bronx. The Public Mission Table can shepherd the parish involvement in community organizations, rooting the life of their people in the bricks and mortar, institutions and neighbors of their turf, signs of God's commitment to human history and its redemption.

The Public Mission Table should organize the response to appeals for disaster relief, advocacy efforts, and other opportunities for social ministry.

Whether it's a massive disaster like Katrina, or earthquakes in some remote corner of the world, or a refugee crisis in the Middle East or unaccompanied minors crossing our southern border, the Public Mission Table should coordinate the response, including funding, education, and if possible, on-site listening and serving opportunities, where lamentations can be heard and solidarity in Christ can be lived.

The Public Mission Table should provide opportunities for education and spiritual formation for parish members.

Service forms faith. It is catechetical. We learn about God, faith and ourselves in the midst of service among and with people who reflect God back to us. Bible studies on aging, hunger, and other issues engaged by the ministry of the parish will undergird these efforts in the world. The action/reflection model of deeper learning has been particularly effective in the parishes I have served. After a stormy meeting with the mayor about the proliferating drug traffic in the neighborhood, people prayed together the story of the removal of a roof in Mark 2 so that this paralysis of their community can come into the midst of their religious assembly. After singing Christmas carols in a nursing home a parish youth group reflects on their experience through the story of Anna and Simeon and the baby Jesus (Luke 2:25 ff.) Support groups are started for the single parents in a parish school and Sunday School, and another for the bereaved in congregation and community. Members about to serve dinner for the homeless for the first time are trained not only by those who already work with the poor, but also with Scripture stories that relate the compassion of Jesus. In short, it is be the task of the Public Mission Table to use the ministries in their oversight as means to increase the faith and effectiveness of the people of God.

The Public Mission Table should initiate one major project each year to expand its mission.

Opportunities for effective mission abound, and may be as varied as our congregations.

- be to host a series of community organization training sessions in the neighborhood, or to send a team to a national community organizing training event
- participate in resettling a refugee
- initiate an interfaith engagement
- participate in or host a homeless ministry
- make a service trip to the southern border with Mexico to listen to the stories of children who fled Central America, and those who help them

The Public Mission Table should link the concerns of the world and the liturgy of the Church.

Through announcements and prayer requests the committee members will bring the practical and human concerns of "seeking the welfare of the city" to each liturgy. One of the most powerful examples of this congruence took place one day in my former parish when we linked the table of the altar with the kitchen table in the house next door that we had purchased to provide shelter for homeless women and children. Our effort to house these children of God caused controversy in the congregation—several members left the parish—and community-zoning laws multiplied as the town actually fought our ministry. Our resolve to sustain this ministry in the face of the deep and visceral opposition was cemented when we connected the tables. After we had received Holy Communion at the altar we processed to the house. The procession went to the kitchen table where the cross and torches illumined groups of members who prayed at the table for the mothers and children who would be living in the house. We then returned to the altar to hear the benediction and the command: "Go in peace, serve the Lord."

The Public Mission Table will remain centered in the Word and Sacraments, extending them into the world, giving shape to Jesus in the ebb and flow of human life. Its witness in the world will point to the destiny of every corporal act of mercy, every corporate act of social justice. Word and Sacrament and Word and service are one thing, the sound of two hands clapping. "Then I saw a new heaven and a new earth... and I heard a loud voice from the throne saying, 'See, the home of God is among mortals. He will dwell with them as their God... he will wipe every tear from their eyes. Death will be no more.'"

POINTS FOR REFLECTION AND DISCUSSION

1. *What scripts in your life and in your church need to be flipped? What would the narrative sound like after the script is flipped?*

2. *What biblical or theological foundation of engagement speaks most directly to you? Why? How do you imagine engaging the world in a different way?*

3. *In what ways are advocacy and mobilization essential tenets of a living a life of faith? What makes advocacy and mobilization sometimes difficult in a congregation? How can those difficulties or obstacles be mitigated?*

CHAPTER SEVEN

CONGREGATIONS AND COMMUNITY ORGANIZING

When the Stranger says, "What is the meaning of this city?
Do you huddle together because you love each other?"
What will you answer? "We all dwell together
to make money from each other"? or "This is a Community"?
T. S. Eliot, "Choruses from The Rock"

Filling the Naked Public Square

To the list of commemorations of heroes of the Church, I would add the name of a radical, feisty Jew: Saul Alinsky. When asked by a group of seminarians for advice for the future, Alinsky said something like: "You only need to answer one question: Do you want to be bishop? All the other answers will follow." (I flunked that quiz). Many years ago I read Alinsky's *Rules for Radicals*, and my world has never been quite the same since. Later Alinsky's legacy was to have a direct influence on my life and ministry in the form of the intelligent, tough, and well-trained organizers he left behind. The discipline and sound activism of community organizing still makes sense to me as a vehicle for real participation of the people of God in the creation of human community. I am more convinced than ever that it provides a means for living the implications of the gospel in today's world.

It has been my privilege to associate with some of the finest organizers around, from all of the major organizing networks, especially those from the Alinsky-founded Industrial Areas Foundation. My ministry from parish pastor to bishop to denominational leader has been in many ways touched and shaped by the discipline and arts of community organizing.

In his book *The Naked Public Square: Democracy and Religion in America*, Richard John Neuhaus wrote about our society being diminished as the "result of political doctrine and practice which would exclude religion and religiously grounded values from the conduct of public business." He argued that the values and beliefs of our Christian traditions have always been a part of the shaping of America and must be returned to the "naked public square." He wrote, "Christian truth, if it is true, is public truth. It is accessible to public reason. It impinges upon public space. At some critical points of morality and ethics it speaks to public policy."

In our time we are seeing what the world looks like when the voice of religion is absent from public debate that is dominated by anger and fear, often exploited by those who would lead us. How does religious truth speak to public policy without crossing the line that separates church and state? I am not talking here about attempts to evangelize in the public square. I'm talking about finding the courage to again speak our truth (the Day Approaching) in the darkness of the A Train hurtling through the dark tunnel. Only in the collective can we find the courage necessary to raise our grace-based voice.

> Only in the collective can we find the courage necessary to raise our grace-based voice.

Can we regular church-goers engage in the negotiations, the compromises, the deals that shape our world, participating with power and skill as we speak from our enduring values? One biblical mandate is as old as creation. Humans were created to "fill the earth and conquer it." To be subjects, not objects of our world, is part of the dignity of being human and honors the Creator. Can not community organization that attempts to involve us in the public square be a form of worship?

The people of God do not often participate in political discourse in meaningful ways. Our denominations do lobby and advocate on certain issues, the important faith practice of advocacy. Our judicatories do pass statements and resolutions in an important expression of our prophetic witness. Both of these practices shape our message and define our voice in the naked public square. But these efforts are often made without any serious intention to develop in the people the kind of power that will make these convictions effective and real in the public square. Community organization is the faith practice that does that.

Community organizing can help the many Christians who call on Jesus and His Church for guidance in finding effective ways to live their faith in public life. Community organizing is not for those who would bask in the ultimate comfort of their virtuous convictions. It is for those with courage to act on their convictions in a faith active in love.

Your Face, Your Cloak, Your Coat, Your Shoes

> "But I say to you, do not resist an evildoer. But if anyone strikes you on the right cheek, turn the other also; and if anyone wants to sue you and take your coat, give your cloak as well; and if anyone forces you to go one mile, go also the second mile."
>
> Matthew 5:39-41

Let's talk about community organization by way of a story which comes to us through Joseph Brodsky, the Soviet émigré, poet and essayist. At seven in the morning a guard in a prison camp of the Russian gulag threw open the door of a cell and addressed the inmates. "Citizens! The collective of this prison's guards challenges you, the inmates, to socialist competition in cutting the lumber piled in our yard."

There was no central heating in that part of Russia. All owners were taxed a tenth of their lumber and it was stored in the prison yard. The need for cutting was evident, yet these "socialist competitions" always brutalized the prisoners.

One of the inmates inquired, "What if I refuse to take part in this?"

"Well, in that case, no food for you," replied the guard.

Axes were issued and the cutting began. Both prisoners and guards worked in earnest and by lunchtime all were exhausted, especially the underfed and overworked prisoners. They all sat down to eat—except for the one who had asked the question. He kept swinging his axe. Guards and prisoners made fun of him. After the break they all kept working. By four in the afternoon the guards' shift ended and they stopped working. A bit later the inmates quit. But they all kept watch as the questioner's axe kept swinging. He was urged to stop by both parties but he would not. He seemed possessed by an inexorable rhythm. At five o'clock, at six, the axe was still violently chopping up and down. All were watching him keenly. The sardonic look on their faces eventually gave way to bewilderment and finally horror. This fool would work himself to death, and none of them wanted any part of it.

"Stop," the other prisoners exhorted. "You will kill yourself." The axe swung on.

"Enough!" the captain of the guard said. "Stop." The lone axman carried on.

Long into the dark the axe swung. Finally, late in the evening, the exhausted man dropped the axe to the ground and staggered to his cell. For the rest of his stay in that prison there were no further calls for socialist competition.

This story moved me powerfully when I first read it. It seems a fitting parable for community organization. This seemingly powerless man found a way to participate in the unfolding destiny of his narrowly circumscribed world. Out of the materials at hand he created power (the ability to act), opposed injustice and made his neighborhood a little better. He went beyond the oft-quoted maxim from the Sermon on the Mount to "turn the other cheek" and acted on the verses which follow, "if any man will...take away thy coat, let him have thy cloak also..." The prisoner had organized the things at hand: his axe, his strength, his dignity, his inner rhythm. He had devised tactics that made a difference, in this case he rendered evil absurd and dwarfed its demands through the excessive volume of his compliance. This apparently powerless victim had managed to expose the vacuity of the entire Soviet enterprise.

The skewed values and shallow beliefs of much of our current mythos in America must be challenged by those who long for signs of God's *shalom*.

The naked public square of American life needs the participation of the people of God. The skewed values and shallow beliefs of much of our current mythos in America must be challenged by those who long for signs of God's *shalom*. Community organization based in parishes and religious institutions of all faiths may bring together the disparate cheeks, coats, cloaks, and pairs of feet that are still capable of going a mile or two farther.

The fundamental elements of a successful organizing effort are well-established, and simple enough:

Institutions. Unlike movements and civic groups and associations open to individual membership, the type of organization I am talking about is institutionally based. These institutions are typically churches, mosques, synagogues, temples, but may include other civic organizations with shared values. An organization of institutions innately has more power and stability than one composed of individuals. This institutional stability and aggregate power provide a firm foundation for individuals and families in those institutions to be effective heroes and leaders in building a just world.

Money. Money is power. It also provides ownership, and the ability to engage the services of the best resources available for training the leadership and consulting on its tasks and actions. The potential economic power of organized institutions can also bring leverage to negotiations. It can keep a branch of a bank in a neighborhood, or lower insurance rates, or leverage equity, for example.

People. A letter to a mayor is one thing. Two thousand organized people at a public negotiating session with that same mayor is something else. Organized people mean power. They can fill an auditorium, a courtroom, a corporate lobby. They vote. Isolated, they are spectators to the making of history. Organized, they realize their scriptural potential to be their sister's and brother's keepers.

Values and Beliefs. Focused conviction can change the world. It has throughout history. Read the Book of Acts. Remember the civil rights movement. At the heart of action are Word and Sacraments. People who believe in the real presence in the bread and wine will yearn for its incarnation in neighbor and community. Churches grow when they invite people to live their beliefs. People want to be part of something which knows what it believes and is serious about living out the implications of those beliefs. In fact, the life of the spectator church becomes mundane, boring, and in danger of losing meaning when people are unwilling or unable to act on what they believe. The man willing to swing an axe to the point of collapse, fueled by his inner hopes and longings, was able to change his little corner of the *gulag*.

It is the hope of parish-based community organization that the fabric of our churches can be organized to become an instrument through which the hopes of God's people can be stretched out into the public life in effective ways.

Principles driving a parish-based community organization

An organization of institutions should be committed to a variety of well-understood and widely agreed upon principles of organizing:

A broad base. It will be ecumenical and interfaith. It will put together different neighborhoods. It will be multi-cultural, multiracial. It will engage the poor and the middle class, blue-state and red-state political instincts.

A collective leadership and commitment to vocation formation. An effective community organization is concerned with the development and empowerment of people. They have an inherent, even primal, commitment to nurture leadership. Such training takes place in the interplay between action and reflection. I have had the privilege to witness many times the process whereby passive citizens, at one time mere spectators in the halls of power, have become effective leaders in the community organizing process. These are some of the people I have watched mature along the way:

- A woman from Queens sits in the office of the Commissioner of Consumer Affairs of New York City and confronts him with specific facts about drugs and pornography unchecked in her community.
- A Catholic sister takes intensive ten-day training in Chicago so that she can learn how to better organize the neighborhood she serves in Pittsburgh.
- A young mission developer, and a young community organizer in Portland, Oregon are creating a new congregation among mostly young people. The terms of engagement are their ongoing participation in a faith-based community organization. There are over fifteen of these new ministry starts among young people—called the "Organizing For Mission Cohort" in the ELCA—using the arts and discipline of community organizing to build new faith communities.

- A housewife in Newark, New Jersey, after being part of a delegation to the Mayor's office, comments that she would previously have never thought herself capable of doing something so significant.
- A retired cop in Baltimore negotiates with the corporate executives to stop bank redlining in his neighborhood.
- An insurance salesman in Chicago negotiates eloquently with a gubernatorial candidate about a toll bridge in his community.
- An Ecuadoran immigrant in Los Angeles meets with a precinct commander about getting rid of drugs in his neighborhood's schools.

These are the little people politicians lie to, the objects of advertiser's hype, the consumers of the myriad solutions of the planners and developers; those who must take it when the subways and buses are overcrowded, garbage piles up, buses break down, crime rises, apartments go condo and the air goes foul. These are the rats put in a maze of planning boards, community relations specialists, and every kind of bureaucratic red tape —all designed to keep people from gaining control of their own destiny.

I have seen people like these become women and men of dignity, courage, and considerable skill. They learn to be resilient, hopeful, and strong. They gird themselves with their faith as they embark on a journey of self-discovery.

A focus on multiple issues. Groups formed around just one issue are properly called movements. They are typically poorly led, ineffectual and temporary. The kind of organization I am describing is neither a single issue movement nor an attempted panacea. A top-flight community organization is an instrument to enable churches, families, and neighborhoods to confront the mix of challenges and issues before them. Citizens' power organizations like these need a healthy blend of local issues, cutting directly to people's self-interests, as well as regional and more broadly corporate issues. Just as community organizations are a real means of entree into the public arena for members, they can also lead them, once organized, to be engaged in the larger peace and justice issues raised by their denominations.

A commitment to action. I remember a meeting in a large New Jersey city about the housing crisis in the face of gentrification. The meeting included presentations by academics, religious leaders, and local activists. As I watched the flow of the meeting it occurred to me that the people who were intensely and passionately participating suffered from the illusion that this meeting was itself a form of action. There was no strategy for empowerment of the neighborhood people and churches to go into action around the issues being passionately discussed. While the meeting seemed cathartic to some, to me it was a waste of time.

Action is the oxygen of any organization. In action leaders emerge, real friends and enemies surface, values are tested, respect is forged, and social change becomes a possibility. Actions—be they Eucharist or Baptism, a mass meeting with a mayor, or a visit to the tax assessor's office to locate owners of abandoned buildings—are the matrix in which faith is formed and fed, evidence of a vibrant hope, signs of the Day Approaching.

Ownership by the people. Hard money, raised and spent by the people themselves, guarantees that they will maintain ownership of their organization. This ownership is a powerful motivating and organizational force. In organizing projects with which I have been associated, the religious institutions raised thousands of dollars of their own money before they sat down with their Church bodies and local businesses to propose funding partnerships. A good example of the power of local ownership of the project comes out of the East Brooklyn Churches organization in New York City. In an area of intense poverty, the people engaged with major denominations, with city, state and federal officials, and with private developers to rebuild their neighborhoods. Project Nehemiah saw 3,000 new homes built on the rubble of a ravaged neighborhood—affordable homes, accessible to local residents. Lutherans put six million dollars of mission money into the finance pool. The Roman Catholics and Episcopalians added many millions more. From the city, EBC negotiated free land, $10,000-15,000 interest free loans, and tax abatements that helped assure affordability. From the state and Governor Mario Cuomo they won permanent financial assistance with ten percent of the mortgage money. To my mind one of the most amazing things that happened was when the Reverend Johnny Ray Youngblood, the pastor of a black Baptist church, presented a special donation to the Catholic and Anglican bishops in attendance at his church. The donation, a check for $100,000, had been raised by 100 of Youngblood's parishioners, each of whom loaned $1,000 to the pastor for Nehemiah Housing at no interest. We are a long way here from denominational paternalism. The white churches got their act together. The black churches got their act together. Each religious institution got its act together. The community moved from strength into the public arena. They showed us all the power of ownership in the process of community building.

We saw that lesson in action more than once in the Metropolitan New York Synod of the Evangelical Lutheran Church of America (ELCA). In the run up to the millennial year of 2000, we were looking for an opportunity to live into the concept of Jubilee, the biblical concept that every 1,000 years there should be economic restoration, with debts forgiven, offering new beginnings for those in debt, especially for the poor and disenfranchised. Faith communities directed a lot of pressure at the International Monetary Fund and the World Bank to forgive the debt of nations living in poverty, helping to lead to the creation of the bank's eight Millenium Development Goals. Four of our congregations serving the poorest in our city owed $1.5 million to our Mission Investment Fund. We decided that we needed a Jubilee in our own house before we could have anything to say to the rest of the world. When asked to forgive the debt, the Mission Investment Fund at first declined. So we adapted the arts of community organizing and invited the leaders of the MIF to New York to meet with local pastors and leaders from these four congregations. They shared their commitment and track record in their communities and congregations.

We launched a campaign to raise half the money ourselves, with a goal of $750,000, won commitments from our presiding bishop and the MIF to match those funds. That local "skin in the game" sealed the deal. Pastors and leaders of the four congregations fanned out into the synod, preaching and sharing testimony. We reached the goal. The finest public community organizing action I have ever attended was the liturgy of celebration for the removal of the debt from these congregations so that they could direct their resources to rebuilding their part of the wall of the city.

A commitment to build real power. Power has been defined as "the ability to act on one's values with effectiveness." Empowering people requires allies, others who share common ground, to break through the wall that separates city from suburb, Geneva from Rome from Jerusalem, poor from middle class, white from black, young from old, immigrants from citizens, men from women, gay from straight. We are too often divided from one another by those who stand to gain from our failure to establish relationships with one another. A new rainbow coalition with muscle can be a new form of ecumenical and interfaith prayer, the offering up of the organized faces, coats, cloaks, and shoes of the people of God for the sake of the world.

A commitment to a reliable organizing network. This sponsoring committee of a faith-based community organization will need to hire a professional organizer to train the leaders of the organization. There is a place for seasoned clergy and laity, and collective leadership is one of the goals and benefits of the process. But the professional trainer plays a critical role. Organizing a community into a solid, responsible, and responsive instrument for social change cannot be left to those among us who have read a few books or led a protest or two. A qualified organizer's support should include regular consultation with on-site staff, continuous opportunities for leadership training and a pool of qualified personnel. There are many organizers around, from many different networks. Good ones are well worth the expense.

A commitment to an ongoing cycle of action, recruitment, negotiation, training, and reflection. Mine is not an appeal to simple activism, but rather for a new way of being in the world. The journey is as crucial as the destination. It is about a communal embrace of our faith and our world on the part of our congregations. "The city needs a soul and the people must give it." We must remember that statement by John Paul II in Yankee Stadium as we go through difficult rites of passage in the public articulation of our faith. It is our hope that the local religious institutions and their families will want to be a part of the work for the soul of the city.

Converging Paths

While in Queens, New York, as a young pastor at Atonement Lutheran Church in Jackson Heights, I was privileged to be a part of the maturing organization of 75,000 families rooted in churches and neighborhoods, an organization of incredible diversity. I saw the Queens Citizen's Organization stand up to the mayor of New York and win on many local issues. I saw them negotiate with the Port Authority of New York and New Jersey and win several million dollars for improvements in neighborhoods in which the authority does business. I saw abandoned buildings again become habitable. I saw QCO cut arson in our borough by thirteen percent (the only borough with a decrease in the city) after a year-long campaign. I saw new signs of hope in old neighborhoods: drug and porn busts, revitalization of business strips, the addition of police precincts, the installation of traffic lights, and similar public safety issues. More importantly, I witnessed the founding of institutionalized relationships with those in power. I saw nothing else during my time in Queens which forged such hope, such deep ecumenical ties, such pride and dignity. Across northern New Jersey we rebuilt our parishes by participating in rebuilding our region, efforts that included affordable housing for seniors, housing for low-income residents, and new beginnings for the homeless.

I am now witnessing such groups, large and small, all across our country, from rural organizing in Indiana to long established organizing efforts in Milwaukee and Chicago. We teach the relational arts of community organizing to mission developers and redevelopers, and use them in the processes of developing Area Mission Strategies. We have a national Community Organizing desk that has sponsored two national training sessions, using trainers from several networks. I see lightbulbs go on when leaders on my staff have participated in such training, especially through the process of "provoking one another to love and good works," described elsewhere in this book. Such training leads to a new-found clarity about values and vocation.

Internal Benefits of Community Organizing

The most important reasons for a congregation to become a part of a church-based community organization are internal. Participation inevitably contributes to the growth and renewal of the congregation, helps forge a new clarity about mission, and encourages the personal development of new leaders. But there are several additional good reasons why I believe that churches, pastors, and denominations ought to consider the converging paths of parish ministry and community organization:

- A grassroots community organization will provide an organized constituency in a given area which can hold accountable the layers of public and private institutions involved in knitting or destroying the fabric of the community. It can develop the power, credibility, and skill to represent the interests of the churches and its families to those in power. And ultimately it can be mobilized for progress in larger issues like immigration reform.
- A grassroots community organization will provide allies to isolated churches and neighborhoods. A church-based community organization can provide the sinew for Area Mission Strategies.
- A grassroots community organization will provide training for a congregation's pastor and leadership: in how to energize the social ministries and evangelism efforts of the parish; how to identify, re-

search, devise tactics, and win on local and regional issues; how to run efficient and effective meetings; how to negotiate both internally and externally; how to proposition others, act on issues, raise money and relate the congregation's faith to its actions in the public arena.

- A grassroots community organization will place the activity of the church in the middle of the world of doubt and struggle, where the mass of unchurched people can come into contact with the love and concern of the people of God. Where new tables in the community can be built, it is a means of evangelization.
- A grassroots community organization will provide an instrument for ecumenical, interfaith and multi-cultural engagement in the life of the overall community. For us Christians it widens the dimension of our living out the meaning and implications of our Baptism and Eucharist.

1. *What does it mean to bring a Christian voice to the public square in a nation that values separation between church and state?*

2. *What do you most need to pay attention to when building collective voice and collective power? What blind spots might your congregation have when constructing new tables in new ways?*

3. *How do you build commitment in a short-term world? What particular challenges do we face now when attention spans in general are so short and problems are so complex?*

4. *What does commitment have to do with hope? What does it have to do with fear?*

CHAPTER EIGHT

INTERFAITH DIALOGUE, RACE, AND IMMIGRATION

NEW TABLES BEYOND ANGER

Interfaith: The Church in America Is a Church on Mars Hill

One afternoon, following a luncheon reception at the Greek Orthodox residence on 79th Street in Manhattan, a number of us clerics spilled out to the sidewalk, looking like the cast from the movie *Men in Black*. As I climbed into a cab the driver stared at me in black suit, clerical collar, and pectoral cross, and inspected the others on the sidewalk, dressed like they'd just been sent over by central casting.

"Are you from the division of Christianity which follows Jesus?" my turbaned driver asked.

I nodded. "Are you a Sikh?" I asked in turn.

"How did you know that?"

"Your turban, the name Singh on your license here, an educated guess. Your Baba of Amritsar was in town last week, right?"

"How did you know that?"

And then he began asking questions. He pulled the taxi over and turned off the meter and asked me about Jesus. Nobody was converting anyone here, but we were showing a little respectful knowledge and sincere curiosity about one another. The common mission to which we Christians are called is that of Saint Paul on Mars Hill. There is such a spiritual hunger in our current culture, just as there was in Athens of old, and so many known and unknown gods that we "ought not to think that the deity is like gold, or silver, or stone, an image formed by the art and imagination of mortals" (Acts 17:29). Paul respected this hunger for spiritual dialogue and engaged it, just as we are all called to respect and engage in it with others today. We have gifts to share, of course, but we also need to be open to receiving the wisdom of other traditions.

A gas station in Queens on December 6, 2001: A man wearing a turban gassed up my car, then handed me a brochure with these words from the Tenth Guru of the Sikhs on the cover: "Recognize ye all human race as one." On an inner panel was a picture of Balbir Singh Sodhi, a Sikh gas station owner murdered four days after 9/11 because his attacker thought he looked like a Muslim. On the back panel was a picture of a little Sikh boy with a turban waving two American flags. My gas station attendant was a neighbor of the church I had just left and though I am sure he is still afraid for his life in today's America, he remains ready to mix his faith with the varying spiritual enchantments of his adopted home. In the days after 9/11, a number of Arab- and Muslim-owned properties in New York were vandalized, and there were many harsh encounters on the streets. But there was a simultaneous, significant effort to protect, support and understand our interfaith neighbors. Both President Bush and Mayor Giuliani showed some of their finest moments of leadership in calling on us to remember that Islam was not our enemy, and urging us not to draw the wrong conclusions. For every rock thrown through a window in New York , a hundred flowers were placed. Muslim and Arab neighbors brought their children to Salaam Arabic Lutheran Church in the Bay Ridge neighborhood of Brooklyn, knowing it would be a safe haven in the crazy days after the attack, as the 2016 presidential campaign was to demonstrate so pointedly. But that interfaith solidarity we discovered in those early weeks following the attack has eroded in the years following the attacks.

The normal—and biblical—situation of Christians throughout the world is as a minority, surrounded by those with cultural and religious differences. This is the context of our discipleship. For the first three centuries Christianity lived as a tiny minority. Outside Europe and the U.S., Christians remain a minority. In Kuala Lumpur, Malaysia, members of the Lutheran Church live their witness in the public space as a minority seeking the best for society in a spirit of cooperation with their Muslim neighbors.

We keep hearing that this or that is not really Islam, this or that is what it really is. The world is ready to ask as well: What is a real Christian?

One Muslim friend of mine is fond of saying: "The only bible many in our society may ever encounter is you." The Constantinian experience of Christendom, where Christianity is the dominant religion of the state, was far from the experience of biblical Christians. Every word of the New Testament assumes Christians live in a world in which most people do not follow Jesus. The events of 9/11 called forth the deep spiritual particularity of the many diverse communions of our spiritual fabric. We yearned for the best, and deepest of our collective soul. For Christians, Jesus and the cross are our guides into the great immensity of this world's enchantment, and the world was opened for us to receive our most truthful expression of community and belief. We keep hearing that this or that is not really Islam, this or that is what it really is. The world is ready to ask as well: What is a real Christian? Today, more than ever, we need to open up new public spaces for interfaith encounter among all of our neighbors, from all the world's religions, and even those who profess no faith at all. But in our particular political and global context today, it means a need for space for partnership with the three Abrahamic faiths: Christians, Jews, and Muslims.

The PRIO conferences described earlier in this book managed to bring together religious leaders, scholars and public servants from the three Abrahamic religions from the U.S. with leaders from Iran in an effort to promote peace between two countries which do not know each other and seemed ready to go to war. I left you in the midst of a sharp exchange with an Ayatollah sitting next to me.

"You Western religionists are not serious," he argued. "You are dilettantes because you would allow God to be mocked."

He referenced Salman Rushdie's book, *The Satanic Verses*, the Copenhagen cartoons depicting Muhammed, and the movie *The Last Temptation of Christ*. I shot back: "We don't understand your *fatwas* condemning people to death for something they said."

He pushed me further and demanded a better answer: "People who mock God are an infection on the life of the faithful, leading people astray, hurting the faith of the common person."

"Interfaith conversation begins with faith." I replied. "If we can see one another through one another's eyes we will gain deeper understanding. There is so much in our religions we share. We agree that Jesus is a great prophet, a holy religious leader. But you will never understand a Christian unless you understand that for Christians Jesus is the very expression of God among us. Truly human, truly God. And you will never understand a Christian unless you understand that it was the very willingness of Jesus to be mocked, to be hurt, to be put to death on the cross...this is very hard to explain...but Christians believe that at the cross, in God's willingness to be vulnerable through Jesus, even to giving his life, that this is in some way the beginning of the peace, reconciliation and renewal of all things, including us."

The next day, during a bus tour of Lisbon, that Ayatollah and some others, including an interpreter, came back to converse with us. He asked, "Why did Jesus have to die on the cross?"

"Do you want the historical reason or the theological reason?" I asked.

"Both," he said.

And for an hour in the back of a bus we talked about the cross of Jesus Christ. Again, no one was converted, but mutual understanding is the birthplace of peace.

This conversation was only possible because the years of interfaith dialogue had moved us from being wary enemies to partners at the table. For many years, the State Department told us, this was the only game in town, a back channel for peace. Our delegation included members of congress, academics, religious leaders from the Abrahamic traditions, seminary presidents, pastors, business leaders, even a couple Roman Catholic cardinals. Iran's delegation continued to grow into the leadership now running the country. A core group of us provided continuity as more voices came to the table. Our own Lutheran presiding bishop, Elizabeth Eaton, was the first head of communion to participate. Politicians and diplomats negotiated the terms of the nuclear agreement eventually enacted, but religious leaders had played a critical role. Religious dialogue and relationship building had helped set the table for the diplomats. The process we engaged in was an off-the-record, safe space for everyone to speak and listen forthrightly.

Rev. Trond Bakkevig, a Norwegian Lutheran pastor, was the moderator for these peace sessions. Writing in the *Practitioner's Report*, published by PRIO, he points out an important take-away from this process:

> The desire and need for religious dialogue and cooperation usually stem from crises, since crises tend to lead to increased religious activity. When people and society experience outside threats, feel insecure, or sense a need for strengthening group identities, there is always an increase in religious activity. This is also why religious leaders have special responsibilities in such situations; religion can be used to exacerbate and deepen conflicts. Therefore, religious leaders must show that religion is not only a refuge, but can also be a source of strength which is needed to take believers on the path to peace.

If we religious leaders want a role in efforts to create peace, we must rise above our own beliefs, history, or national politics, secure in them but ready to go beyond them to listen and learn from others. Here is a summary of guidelines that Pastor Bakkevig drew from these conferences that are relevant for interfaith encounters in our communities as we progress through religious conflicts and misunderstandings.

- Religious leaders must be secure in their own identity in order to be able to recognize, respect, and appreciate the religious faith of followers of another religion. Even as we bear witness to our own truth, we must be able to listen to the faith of the other. We must have an appreciation of how religion is intertwined with the identity of their people, their tribe, their nation, or their state.
- Religious leaders should refrain from claims of superior access to the mind of God. That does not mean that we do not speak our truth, as revealed to us, but it does mean we recognize that we do not possess truth in its totality. Such humility enables us to listen, and to have dialogue faith to faith.
- We come to the table as interpreters of our own religious texts. Here is where discerning wisdom is needed from our leaders. The Bible offers arguments for war, conflict, and leaves little room for other faiths, but the same Scriptures also teach respect, peace, forgiveness, and reconciliation. We can escalate conflict by emphasizing divisive elements of our sacred texts, or we can lift up irenic and graceful elements of our particular faiths. This does not mean that we do not face conflicts with one another forthrightly. Religious leaders have a special responsibility for identifying religiously charged elements of a conflict. They should provide a theological understanding about why and how these elements are charged, and seek possible solution. In dialogue between Muslims and Christians in many communities the idea of jihad, for instance, must be brought out into the open, so that Muslim leaders can explain the concept in the Koran them-

selves, not leave it to the imagination or faulty understanding of those who are not Muslim.

- When religious leaders enter dialogue, internal discipline is critical. Public statements must not be made unilaterally, but should be mutually crafted.
- Although Chatham House Rules prevailing allowed for some safe off-the-record space in the Iranian dialogue, in general it was understood that the dialogue has to be made public. The Naked Public Square needs witnesses to spiritual depth and community-building wisdom. People need to see religious leaders talking and acting together and identifying mutual acts of mercy.

Race: Reparations and Jubilee

The idea that you are reborn anew, without your history, without being dogged by your past, without who you were haunting you and you having to deal with that, is uniquely American. In America, we have difficulty with acknowledging the fact that where we are in a particular moment is irrevocably tied to our past. We have great difficulty in doing that when it challenges us.

Ta-Nehisi Coates

On the Day of Atonement you shall sound the trumpet throughout all your land. You shall make the fiftieth year holy, and proclaim liberty throughout the land to all its inhabitants. It shall be a jubilee to you; and each of you shall return to his own property, and each of you shall return to his family. That fiftieth year shall be a jubilee to you. In it you shall not sow, neither reap that which grows of itself, nor gather from the undressed vines. For it is a jubilee; it shall be holy to you. You shall eat of its increase out of the field. In this Year of Jubilee each of you shall return to his property.

Leviticus 25

Seventeen years ago, Amadou Diallo was killed in a hail of forty-one bullets from police guns in the Soundview section of the South Bronx, holding a wallet, not a gun, in his hand. Bruce Springsteen wrote a song about it, "41 shots...American Skin." When I wrote an editorial about it, it got me in a lot of trouble. I said that if Amadou had been my son (one of my sons was Amadou's age), he would still be alive. I called on public and religious leaders to admit that we have a racial problem in our community and that we needed to find the resolve to face it together.

Some who disagreed with my remarks threatened to boycott my previously planned visit to a congregation on Long Island whose membership included many New York City police officers and their families. I asked the pastor to read a letter to the congregation the week before my visit in which I asked them to welcome me as a brother in Christ and as their bishop, and I promised to stay at the coffee hour until the last person said what they had to say.

The church was packed for my visit. The congregation was incredibly gracious and hospitable, but there was no way around facing the anger. I stayed a long time. I faced people who took from my public statements that I was accusing the police of racism and murder. There were primal screams from police wives whose husbands had been shot in the line of duty.

But we listened and we stayed in the conversation. They heard from me that during my twenty years of parish ministry I was a police chaplain, and that the cries of mothers whose children were shot by police were remarkably similar to theirs. I learned from them that there is no short cut to engaging one another, to facing our history in this country, especially our original sin of slavery and racism.

The public furor, demonstrations, arrests, the acquittal of those who shot Amadou, the ensuing anger, grief and communal helplessness presaged Ferguson, Baltimore, Charlestown, Dallas, Baton Rouge and so many other confrontations between police and minorities today.

For example, the video of the 2014 shooting of Laquan McDonald by a Chicago police officer was not released until after the re-election of Rahm

Emmanuel as Chicago's mayor. What the video revealed was not just an execution of a young black male, but an administration willfully keeping it under wraps. The reaction was explosive. People took to the streets. Protests went on for days. Chicago ended up with a new police commissioner. The mayor is still in trouble. This was one link in a long chain stretching across the country.

Brenda Smith, now Director for Faith Practices in the Evangelical Lutheran Church in America (ELCA) but then a pastor in an African American congregation and community in Queens, New York, recently looked back on her time there and said, "We will never get anywhere, we won't settle this, if we don't see each other's humanity." Her congregation reached out to their local precinct as they had been doing long before Amadou was shot. They baked and delivered cookies to the precinct before and after the death of Amadou. We persuaded Attorney General Elliott Spitzer to convene a meeting in her church between police and young African American males tired of being profiled. There is no substitute or short cut from the hard work of bringing people together at the table. Peace and reconciliation require a long game. Today, Brenda is leading an effort to encourage every one of our congregations to reach out to their local law enforcement precinct. I joined our leaders in a memorial in Dallas for police officers who were killed there. I have also been with our leaders in places where young black males were killed by law enforcement. At the site of the killing of Alton Sterling in Baton Rouge, we prayed with many neighbors, then were reminded by a street preacher: "Jesus did not call disciples to babysit buildings or guard offerings." Today, we are being called to the street.

Our Churches, including the ELCA, have benefitted institutionally and as individuals from the plunder of African Americans and their property in the history of the U.S. Not only in the past, but continuing into the present, our members and congregations have moved away from African-American neighborhoods (and Latino and other poverty stricken neighborhoods) because we did not want to live with the people who were moving in. We left the church buildings, the debt, and the upkeep, the deteriorating neighborhoods, the draining of jobs and economic capital. Now gentrification threatens to plunder anew the lives and property of people in poverty.

Ta-Nehisi Coates, a frequent writer on race and race relations, and a senior editor for *The Atlantic*, calls for reparations, a concept that has been around for a long time. I remember the Young Lords occupying congregations in East Harlem fifty years ago. They would demand that the Church make reparations to the community they had ignored or exploited. I agree with the concept, but I fear the perceived guilt-tripping is probably a nonstarter in engaging the heart of a mostly white middle class Church body.

As the ELCA continues to wrestle with issues of racial justice and the consequences of our own history, we should declare a Jubilee and reinvest in the ELCA congregations and their communities of color and poverty. A place to begin, in the 96% white ELCA, is to open up space among the 96% to consider race in all the decisions we make in the light of the Gospel. We need to reinvest in meaningful ways in the 4% of our members who are not white. Let the first fruits of the Congregational Renewal effort of the Campaign for the ELCA be used to strategically reinvest in congregations from our ELCA ethnic communities in these neighborhoods. Synods, bishops, and their Renewal Tables, in partnership with ELCA ethnic communities, could identify strategic congregations, present and potential leaders, and achievable area strategies. More broadly, across the Protestant/Roman Catholic spectrum, can we imagine a Jubilee, a reinvestment in our congregations, schools, and institutions in neighborhoods we have abandoned?

> Can we imagine a Jubilee, a reinvestment in our congregations, schools, and institutions in neighborhoods we have abandoned?

But first, we need to open up spaces to hear one another, to face our history, to deepen relationships, so that we can leave our defended spaces, which are shrouded by fear and anxiety, which are too often exacerbated and exploited by our leaders and pundits. And we need to integrate into our communal experiences of racial tragedy the narrative of hope, reconciliation and restoration that is let loose in the world through the death and resurrection of Jesus.

For example, in 2016, nine people were killed at a Bible study at Mother Emmanuel Church (AME) in Charleston, South Carolina. This tragedy is especially disconcerting to my Church body (ELCA) because the killer was a member of one of our congregations, and two of the pastors studied at one of our seminaries. Lutheran and AME congregations in South Carolina are now meeting together for worship and prayer, viewing the movie *Selma* together, and discussing its implications for our life together today.

The Public Mission Table of our congregations can help church members engage in racial justice in sharing the spiritual journeys of their neighbors of other races, sharing in their struggle for justice over the centuries, and in moving out into the public arena together with ministries of advocacy, community organizing, economic development, direct services and other ways to signal the Day Approaching in the public arena.

Congregations and religious institutions can grow in their own journeys of racial justice. Race Forward, an organization dedicated to helping advance racial justice in the world, has offered some helpful ways to think about this.

One is the concept of "equity." How does our organization or congregation advance the cause of racial equity in every decision it makes? This is a way to move beyond individual commitments, attitudes, and insight into the issues. Equity looks at the institutional life of an organization, the way that privilege and practice can get in the way of racial justice. What are our corporate behaviors, habits, blind spots? How do we need to change our way of being in the world, not just as caring individuals, but as organizations? We can examine every aspect of the life of a congregation through this lens of equity.

The other is the concept of "choice points," recognizing moments of opportunity that we may have been oblivious to previously. We can look at most of the decisions we make as opportunities to change the system, move forward on racial equity, or other issues at the heart of our organizations. Creating a budget is a choice point. When we can decide how money will be spent, and how we will invest, we should make decisions that support, for example, a growth in inclusivity of our leadership, or in improving the lives and opportunities for children living in poverty in our community. Another choice point is our hiring process. Aren't those moments of opportunity to advance racial and gender equality?

Finally, let me take you back to my earlier description of the demonstration at our church-wide offices, and the "die in" demonstration, the reading of the names of African Americans killed by police, and the ensuing conversations we were able to have. It is absolutely imperative that public space is opened up so that the bred-in-the-bone wounds of slavery and racism in our country, the inheritance of every human being in America, can be part of the mutual listening and lamentation at every table in the Church and in the world.

Immigration: What Rough Beast Slouching from Ground Zero?

> Come to me, all you that are weary and are carrying heavy burdens, and I will give you rest. Take my yoke upon you, and learn from me; for I am gentle and humble in heart, and you will find rest for your souls. For my yoke is easy, and my burden is light.
> Matthew 11:28-30

> Send these, the homeless, tempest-tossed to me,
> I lift my lamp beside the golden door.
> Emma Lazarus, "The New Colossus"

A freezing rain whipped in on the wind from New York Harbor as we gathered at the Battery in lower Manhattan. Through bone-chilling sleet we could see the lady in the harbor, an enduring iconic presence holding aloft the welcoming torch. It was the day after the President George W. Bush's State of the Union Address in 2006, and New York's religious leaders and immigration advocates were holding a press conference to urge the president and congress to enact humane immigration reform and to reject current legislation pending in Congress that would criminalize acts helping undocumented neighbors.

Just a few blocks away, on a beautiful September day five years earlier, the Twin Towers had come tumbling down, destroying the lives of thousands. For a brief moment afterwards, the world's attention and our own was focused on what mattered most: our shared humanity, our communal compassion, our deepest spiritual longings and hope. But, too soon, all that changed. In the ripples of 9/11, something ugly has emerged, slouching from Ground Zero: a hardening of the heart toward the stranger among us.

We became fearful, and in our fear we came to believe that our security can only be achieved through power, enforcement, a closing of the ranks, and a sealing of our borders. On this cold, rainy day, representatives from many religious traditions gathered to refute that belief and to give voice to a shared spiritual conviction that our mutual security is tied not to power and isolation, but to the well-being and dignity of every child of God. We were gathered to ask our president, our leaders, and our fellow citizens: What kind of community is emerging from Ground Zero? What kind of communal future are we building together?

> Mere anarchy is loosed upon the world,
> The blood-dimmed tide is loosed, and everywhere
> The ceremony of innocence is drowned;
> The best lack all conviction, while the worst
> Are full of passionate intensity...
> And what rough beast, its hour come round at last,
> Slouches toward Bethlehem to be born?
> William Butler Yeats, "The Second Coming"

What kind of a world is aborning in the changed communal land-scape following 9/11, a world where the rough beast of fearful exclusion slouches across landscapes both here and abroad?

We are having the wrong conversation in our country about immigration today. It is a conversation driven by fear and often cynically manipulated by our political leaders for partisan gain. Yes, security is important, but at what price? How much are we willing to pay for the illusion that we can ever be totally secure? How many walls can we build? Politicians play cynically on our fears that our most serious threat is from migrants and asylum seekers. Where is moral, political, and religious leadership? It is far too easy to bypass legitimate concerns about the world we are building together and too quickly play the role of policy wonks, divided by this or that proposal or legislative agenda.

The Church is too often silent as politicians build public constituencies on visceral communal uneasiness and fear of the stranger. Our Church bodies pass public statements on immigration while we ignore opportunities for real conversation. We talk about "them" as if they were faceless, voiceless beings, forgetting—perhaps by choice—that they, too, are children of God. The global debate over immigration, economic migration, and a new emerging America is begging for Christian insight, faith, and bold ideas. This book proposes to be an entry into that larger and better conversation.

Scripture is not ambiguous about this issue. We may be divided on how to sort out the immigration mess we are in today, but, when the stranger knocks at the door, people of the Book instinctively open their door and attend to the immediate needs of the other. As Martin Luther noted, when hospitality is given to the persecuted and oppressed, "God Himself is in our home, is being fed at our house, is lying down and resting"

> The global debate over immigration, economic migration, and a new emerging America is begging for Christian insight, faith, and bold ideas.

Like our daughter Rachel, who gleefully announced "I found us!" after discovering our family name among the endless list of immigrant names on the wall at Ellis Island, in welcoming the stranger we may well find ourselves again as a nation and a Church of immigrants. Unless our forebears were here already as Native Americans, or came by the middle passage of slavery, Rachel's discovery belongs to all of us.

I often say that we Christians are followers of Jesus and therefore must be pro-immigrant because Abraham, a wandering Aramean, was our grandfather in the faith, and his wife, Sarah, is our grandmother.

> **A wandering Aramean was my father...he went down into Egypt and lived there as an alien, few in number. When the Egyptians treated us harshly we cried to the Lord, the God of our ancestors, and he brought us out with a mighty hand and brought us into this place and gave us a land flowing with milk and honey.**
>
> **Deuteronomy 26:5-8**

An economic migrant, a desert nomad leads his family toward a land of promise. "Now the Lord said to Abram, "go from your country and your kindred and your father's house to the land that I will show you" (Genesis 12:1). And so begins the great trek for new life, survival, redemption. He will also find danger enough that he plans to pass his wife off as his sister. It is a trek repeated in the heat of the Sonoran desert, in boats from Africa running ashore in southern Europe, in the hulls of boats from Fujian provinces to the shores of Long Island.

Along the trek Abram finds hope, welcome, signs from God. At each place of hope and refreshment he builds an altar and calls on the name of God. He named these places of remembrance of God's grace on his journey with names like Shechem and Bethel. "Abram passed through the land to the place at Shechem...Then the Lord appeared to Abram and said: 'To your offspring I will give this land.' So he built there an altar to him" (Genesis 12:6-7).

Shechem today looks a lot like a warm cot in the undercroft at Gloria

Dei Lutheran Church in Long Island, giving shelter to migrant workers in winter; it looks like Lutheran congregations along *la frontera* in Texas reaching out to migrant workers on both sides of the border; it looks like the *amigos en pie* immigrant ministry of Trinity Lutheran Church on 100th Street in Manhattan, immigrants helping immigrants; Shechem looks like those organized in Amagansett on the east end of Long Island, listening to the stories of those economic migrants rousted out of their homes in the middle of the night; Shechem looks like our congregations in Brooklyn and Los Angeles involved in the sanctuary movement and offering hospitality and safety to vulnerable families. It looks like the hundreds of new immigrant ministries of the ELCA. Bethel. Shechem. A trail of altars. A wandering Aramean is our grandfather in the faith. We are followers of Jesus and descendants of immigrants and refugees.

Our grandfather was a wandering Aramaean. "I found us," my daughter Rachel said on Ellis Island. We find ourselves as we read of Abram's migration, the beginning of our family journey. The altars at which we all worship on the Lord's Day are our Shechem and Bethel, places of refreshment and hope. We find ourselves in each of our new neighbors. *"The alien who resides with you shall be to you as the citizen among you; you shall love the alien as yourself, for you were aliens in the land of Egypt"* (Leviticus 19:33-34).

Maybe that's where we start as we dig into this issue in ecumenical and interfaith partnerships. The issues are complex. But all agree America's immigration system is broken. But Christians have a two-handed God. In the kingdom of the left hand there are many proposals for comprehensive immigration reform and we struggle with others of good will with a humility that we might be wrong about this or that approach, that what we actually can achieve may fall short of our hopes. In the kingdom of the left hand, as we look at comprehensive immigration reform, we enter the fray with a few guiding principles.

We can agree on these principles and disagree on this or that policy in the kingdom of the left hand. Not so, in the kingdom of the right. Red and blue state people sit together in our pews and hear the God of the bible call us to welcome the stranger, care for the neighbor, without equivocation or apology. Compassion, solidarity and generosity of spirit come naturally to grandchildren of a wandering Aramean. You can't love God and not love those whom God embraces. The one who washes our windows, drives the taxi, cares for many of our children, cuts the lawn and washes the dishes, including many new immigrant Christians, is a wandering Aramean. So also our accountants, our technical experts, our elected leaders, our pastors.

Over the years, as Lutheran Immigration and Refugee Service has evaluated various proposals for reform of the immigration system, it has settled on four criteria reflecting our core spiritual values.

Does the proposal promote family unity?

From ICE raids in Postville, Iowa and across the country, to the backlog of family visas where families wait up to fifteen years to be legally reunited, families are being torn apart by our broken system.

> Now there was a man in Jerusalem called Simeon, who was righteous and devout. He was waiting for the consolation of Israel; and the Holy Spirit was upon him. It had been revealed to him by the Holy Spirit that he would not die before he had seen the Lord's Christ. Moved by the Spirit, he went into the temple courts. When the parents brought in the child Jesus to do for him what the custom of the Law required, Simeon took him in his arms and praised God.
>
> Luke 2:25-28

Focus on the hands of an old man, the hands of a grandpa. And think about the hands of the mother. Father David Garcia is the pastor of San Fernando Cathedral in San Antonio, Texas. He described how his Mexican-American community celebrates the Festival of the Presentation. The key is the hands of the mother, *La Virgen de la Candelaria*, the Lady of the

Candles. In one hand she holds a lighted candle, in the other the Christ child. Themes of Epiphany light and the Presentation of Jesus in the temple come together.

At the Presentation Candelaria Mass the priest blesses three things brought from home to church by each family. He blesses the candles which will be used at the home altars for family devotions. It's really a blessing of the kitchen tables of each family of the parish. The altar is a table to unite the tables and the families. Our eating and drinking at each table is a united, holy thing. So he blesses the candles. Then he blesses the *niños*, figures of the Christ child from the family crèche. Then the priest blesses the flesh-and-blood infants and children. The connections between the altar table and the kitchen table, between the Christ child and all children, between the church and the home and the world are beautifully woven into the celebration of the Presentation. Here is the great richness of parish and family life.

The Presentation flows from the Incarnation of Jesus, the Word taking flesh in the world, in a family. Consider all the incredible richness of parish and family life which is brought together in the Presentation story from the Gospel of Luke. In the presence of Jesus and his parents, and his growing extended family in the temple, we call for immigration reform which protects precious families and keeps them together.

Does the proposal promote human rights and worker rights?

Migrant workers come to the United States so they can work, but too often they also experience lower wages, exploitative labor practices, dangerous working conditions, and constant fear and insecurity. Providing legal documents for honest, hardworking migrants would discourage such abuses of human rights and worker rights.

Two decades ago, dozens of deaf mutes in Jackson Heights, Queens, dubbed *los muditos*, were forced to sell trinkets on subways and were beaten regularly if they did not make their quota or tried to escape. Their undocumented status made them vulnerable to exploitation. They lived in virtual slavery because they had no legal status and could easily be jailed and deported back to the hunger and poverty from which they had come. I have met Fujianese workers held in slavery until they paid off their debts for transportation from China to America. Asian and Eastern European young women are enslaved by global sex trafficking. Filipino and African domestic workers have been held as slaves for years in the homes of wealthy people from their own country living in America. Where there is no legal document, families are separated, and workers are indentured and abused without rights or recourse.

Does the proposal enable those without status to come out of the shadows and live without fear?

The vast majority of the twelve million undocumented people living in the United States are otherwise law-abiding, honest, hard-working people who want to provide for themselves and their families. Newcomers without legal immigration documents are among the most vulnerable we are called to care for. By bringing people out of the shadows of fear and marginalization, we allow our immigrant communities to live in the light of liberty, contributing more freely to our culture and economy.

Does the proposal provide for a path to permanence, so that the immigrant can become a full member of society?

Throughout its history, a great strength of the United States has been its welcome to immigrants, manifested by the desire and expectation that immigrants will become citizens and thus fully-participating members of civic society. This tradition has meant that the United States has avoided having a permanent underclass of people of foreign origin who do not share the same rights, and who thus are more subject to discrimination and exploitation.

When the leaders and pastor of the recently closed Salem Lutheran

Church in Bay Ridge, Brooklyn handed the keys, the checkbook, the registry of the congregation and its 103 years of pastoral acts to Pastor Khader El Yatim and the leaders of newborn Salaam Arabic Lutheran Church, a people in exile received a path to permanence and full inclusion. A Lutheran immigrant church welcomes immigrants. Salem begets Salaam, not a sullen minority being forced out of their church in a changing neighborhood, but free and faithful Lutherans from two very different cultures, sharing immigrant roots, taking the time and supreme effort to fall in love with another set of table companions in all of such love's vulnerability. A path to permanence and inclusion is not just a legislative value, but a spiritual gift.

The folks at Salem said, "take care of our heritage," and the folks at Salaam replied "the church you cared for is in good hands." These brothers and sisters walked through the pain and exhilaration of letting go of the familiar and the comfortable and being grasped in the transforming power of the gospel. In some sense it is a reminder that every congregation must always be accepting the invitation to the funeral of the church it remembers even as it is called at the Water Gate to tell the old, old story and share portions with those for whom nothing has been prepared. A path to permanence. Salem speaks Salaam to its new neighbors.

1. *Does your congregation actively engage in interfaith dialogue? If so, how and where? If not, where might you begin and why?*

2. *How does one engage in interfaith dialogue authentically without losing your own unique faith voice? What happens when your perspective changes, is altered by an engagement with different, even alien, points of view?*

3. *How can churches help make conversations about race less scary? What about our liturgical practices can we use to help keep fear of tough conversations at bay?*

4. *How do we work against feelings of guilt in preference for framing difficult conversations like those about complicity and privilege? How would that shift open up conversations, change their contour?*

5. *How do we celebrate commonality without undermining uniqueness?*

CHAPTER NINE

RESURRECTION

You shall be called healers of the breach,
restorers of streets to live in.

Isaiah 58:14

He has lifted up the lowly;
he has filled the hungry with good things.

Luke 1: The Magnificat

Strangers on the Road...Healers of the Breach

Here is the human face of tragedy. Two friends are walking home to Emmaus two days after the great tragedy (see Luke 24: 13-27). They are dazed, their conversation registers disbelief as they nod their heads in shock, talking about the loss of their friend, their hopes. Their world was so upside down that they did not recognize the stranger joining them on the road of sorrow. These friends are in shock. They have lost their integration of faith and life, of history and hope. They cannot yet see resurrection looming over this tragic Friday. The stranger does not confront them, but instead draws them out. "What were you talking about? What things happened in Jerusalem today?" They pour out their lament to the stranger. They arrive at their home and invite the stranger to enter. Word and bread and wine and the presence of the stranger eventually set their broken hearts aflame. They recognize resurrection. The Risen Lord is the bottom line.

It is important to remember the arc of tragedy in the issues coming into view in this book. We began at Ground Zero, the tragedy of September 11, 2001, and we went through the many common tragedies and challenges our congregations have faced since then—both natural and human-made, both in the United States and throughout the world. We cannot deny that our world changed. Distrust between religions has deepened. Attitudes toward immigrants and refugees have hardened. Racial divides have deepened. Wars unleashed by 9/11 have brought episodic terror attacks into our daily landscape of fearfulness. These wars have forced millions on the move, running for their lives, the waves of migrants and refugees spilling into Europe and Texas and across the globe. People are killing each other in the name of religion in Nigeria, the Central African Republic, Bangladesh. A proposed mosque causes the community to react in fear, distrust, and anger. Natural disasters, exacerbated by climate change and the continued pillaging of our environment, continue to grow stronger and more destructive. And chronic disasters of our own manufacture continue, like the unabated violence killing the children in my city of Chicago every single day. Anger, fear, paralysis: That is our public mood. These large communal disasters inevitably feed into the mood of our congregations. Our churches are dwindling, many losing an emerging generation in its entirety. Hunger and poverty and homelessness in our cities and communities seem persistent and intractable.

All of these ground zeros are traced on our foreheads with ashes every year: "Remember that you are dust, and unto dust you shall return." Lamentations everywhere. Yet we have been baptized for this moment. This is the world where grace, which is all around us, albeit sometimes like a dimly burning wick, will not be quenched.

What, then, are we to do?

The boulder of tragedy plunges into the water. Calvary. The Cross. First we must attend to the concentric ripples on the surface. We join our dazed friends on the road—not where we want them to be, but where they are. We draw them out. What things did you see, hear, feel, lose? We attend to their immediate material, spiritual, and psychic needs. We begin to respond to their despondent spirits. All this takes time. We must not dance in the sunshine while they are in the cave. At the end of the mourner's path is God, as the psalmist has promised: *"Where can I go from your Spirit? If I descend to Sheol you are there."* Always present is the Word, the narrative of faith; bread and wine; prayer and liturgy; objective reality not dependent on how we feel today. It takes time, sure, but as we continue to show up, to attend to the sorrow, to comfort and heal and renew, the face of the stranger slowly becomes familiar. Grace comes back into view. Resurrection beckons. The life of faith is a marathon, not a sprint. We cannot force hope; we can only experience it in God's good time. And sometimes we walk the path in both roles: the comforting stranger who shows up on the road and, simultaneously, the dazed and wounded mourner on the cusp of the tragedy, trying to find a way home.

In Galatians. Paul gives insight into this dual role of caregiver and receiver. *"Bear one another's burdens, and in this way you will fulfill the law of Christ...for all must carry their own loads"* (6:2, 5). Carry our own load. No one has the right in the Christian community to expect to have their burdens borne as entitlement. Yet when we carry burdens for one another, grace abides: refreshing and unconditional.

This is the outline of disaster response for our congregations: Show up. Attend first to the ripples on the surface. Accompany the pain on the road. Respond, rescue, reach out, call, pray, touch, embrace, feed, shelter, cry, reassure. Stay in touch with the resources of faith, keep the fires of hope burning even if there seems no possibility of comprehension or integration of experience and spiritual hope. Strangers begin to join us on the road: those who have experienced these things before; those whose vocations are to respond and rescue and organize. Excellence, experience, empathy, resources, and grounded faith walk with us until we can experience and reclaim those gifts for ourselves. Then, and only then, can we begin to organize for the long haul. Gather resources. Work with existing networks in the public, private, and non-profit arenas. Strengthen our mediating institutions—church, congregation, community, family—for the long journey ahead. Tell our stories, lift up our heroes, do communal exegesis, work with the faith community toward discerning spiritual meaning, resurrecting hope, recognizing pervasive grace.

A Short Exegesis of Isaiah 58

> **The Lord will guide you continually and satisfy your needs in parched places, and make your bones strong; and you shall be like a watered garden, like a spring of water whose waters never fail. Your ancient ruins shall be rebuilt. You shall raise up the foundation of many generations. You shall be called the repairer of the breach, the restorer of streets to live in.**
>
> **Isaiah 58: 11-12**

It takes time. Isaiah 58 offers powerful words of hope and resurrection to the ruined city. But remember that the city was indeed ruined in the first place, occasioning the bitter and angry lamentations many centuries before: "*How lonely sits the city that was once full of people; how like a widow she has become...is it nothing to all you who pass by?*" (See Lamentations 1:1, 12.) The demand that God and all those who pass by pay attention was a lament carried on from generation to generation.

Only now, in Isaiah 58, is the beginning of the healing response. The author of this text addresses the community of Israel, who had finally returned from exile in Babylon. The message encourages the community to rebuild the walls and the ruined streets of a ravished Jerusalem and surrounding neighborhoods, but it reminds them to also be concerned with rebuilding faithful commitment to worship and ethical life of the covenant. We have been at that wall in our own times, in our own congregations, as each of us has helped to rebuild the part of the wall nearest to us. But together we have rebuilt the city and renovated our covenant faith, fulfilling the prophets promise: *"You shall raise up the foundation of many generations."*

Every human tragedy, every earthly catastrophe, every wrongful death, every beleaguered immigrant and displaced refugee, calls the question on our priorities, the strength of our communities, the depth of our spiritual resolve to be *"healers of the breach, restorers of streets to live in."* "Healers of the breach" is the long-term ministry which rides the percussive waves beneath the surface, long-term issues of justice, renewal, solidarity, the well-being of every child of God. "Healers of the breach" is the ministry of the spiritual tide beneath the surface; it is the ebb and flow of the resurrection power of the Prince of Tides.

The burning question for us as we draw to the end of this book is whether our congregations are prepared and worthy to stand in unity and justice with others when God appears and Zion is restored. Can we become fully servants of the holy God?

Calls and Letters

When tragedy strikes, you get a lot of calls and advice. The best counsel I got just after 9/11 came from Rev. Rick Foss, a North Dakota bishop who had been a leader in helping set up the response to the flooding in the Red River Valley in 1997, a tragedy in which churches and homes were destroyed, lives were lost, and deep and lingering economic devastation was wrought. He called the day after the tragedy and said, "This is not a time to ask permission, get opinions, consensus. Help the people immediately.

Spend the money you need to spend. Your pastors and people need you now. The city needs a strong Church responding vigorously. Be a leader. You are doing this for all of us. Roll the dice. Count on us. We are in this together."

Bishop Foss's check was one of the first of thousands of dollars I received from the churches of his synod to be used at my discretion. His advice was priceless. His presence on the road reminded me that we were not the first to experience tragedy, that there was a body of knowledge and resilient experience ready to join us. His council of boldness and his pushing me to lead strengthened my weak knees and restored my shattered resolve. His show of material support pointed me in the direction of trust in God's abundance in a time of scarcity and spiritual doubt. We *can* do this for one another. And Bishop Foss helped me to find the central focus of my unfolding ministry: take care of caregivers, be a servant to the Church, and count on others to help.

We received many calls, letters, cards, and emails like his. People expected me to keep a list, encourage a ministry of prayer. Strangers on the road needed company. It became my work of leadership in the community of Jesus to place the fringe of the garment of the Church on the road where those reaching out for consolation and connection could touch it. In my online journal I asked for stories and accounts of people's losses. We collected the names, we prayed frequently and fervently for these dear faces known to us, even as we prayed equally hard for all affected by the tragedy. The Lutheran Counseling Center had an 800 number available to the public just hours after the downtown attacks. It logged hundreds, then thousands of calls a day, another fringe of the garment of Jesus on the road.

I got an early phone call on the first Sunday after the September 11 attacks from our daughter, Rachel: "Dad, I'm outside the church and I'm afraid to go in. It's my first time teaching Sunday School. What will I say to the children? I don't know what to tell them."

Rachel at that moment was every person of faith in our metropolis on that Sunday morning. I told her to go in and just be with the children.

They needed her to be herself, whatever she was feeling or able to say. They needed to be loved, heard, touched. They needed the company of their elders. I wanted to reach through the phone and hold her, this child of mine dazed on the road. It reminded me that although 9/11 wounded all of us, we were yet called to be present and speak a healing word to our wounded communities and the world beyond. It gave me comfort that in a time of few words Rachel's would be in the company of objective things: the faithful community, bread and wine and Word conveying God's promises, the resilience of children. The children would probably not remember a word she said to them, but they would remember that she was there and they would draw comfort from how she was with them on their own road to Emmaus. This is what our Global Mission Partners call "accompaniment," the mission posture of presence and profound respect and love for our partners.

Cruciform Rising

> Do you not know that all of us who have been baptized into Christ Jesus have been baptized into his death? Therefore we have been buried with him by baptism into death, so that, just as Christ was raised from the dead by the glory of the Father, so we too might walk in newness of life. For if we have united with him in a death like his, we will certainly be united with him in a resurrection like his.
>
> Romans 6:3-5

Years before 9/11, when visiting our son, Timothy, in the Peace Corps in Ukraine where he and his wife Erin were teaching, I met a wonderful woman named Nina. She was a fellow teacher, and her husband had been an officer in the Soviet Army. Things were tough economically for everyone at the time. "It's our reality," she would shrug as she spoke of long breadlines, no jobs, electrical black outs, rising crime. She was raised on Soviet atheism and taught to be cynical of any sign of religious faith. She knew I was a pastor. She had sized me up and apparently decided I seemed like a regular guy and not a religious fanatic or someone who would fall for irrational answers to deep questions. Nina was disenchantment personified. One day she looked at me and simply said: "Really, I mean really. Do you really believe all this religious stuff? Really! What do you believe? Do you really think there *is* more after death? I mean really!" Well, that is the big question isn't it?

I brought Nina's question to Ground Zero with me. At that hellish place for the first time, breathing lightly through my mask to mitigate the odor of the death of my sisters and brothers, the furious grinding of gears and metal of the rescue effort all around me, I contemplated the obscene rubble and groped for something, anything to give me consolation. I had pictures in my mind of people I knew to be buried in that mess. There is no happy little ending one can tack onto that.

There was this, which came to me as a gift. I remembered my grandfather, a pastor and seminary teacher of the New Testament, fishing with me when I was about eight years old. He looked at me and said: "Stephen, the only death you have to be afraid of is already behind you in your baptism." And then he went on fishing. He was with me at the pile as I remembered my baptismal answer to Nina's question.

It was this: we have already been buried alive: *Do you not know that all of us who have been baptized into Christ Jesus have been baptized into his death? Therefore we have been buried with him by baptism into death, so that, just as Christ was raised from the dead by the glory of the Father, so we too might walk in newness of life. For if we have united with him in a death like his, we will certainly be united with him in a resurrection like his* (Romans 6:3-5).

Tragedy causes us to question and speak of ultimate things even when there are no immediate or apparent answers. But we are baptized for those moments.

The End of the Story

On March 10, 2002, six months after the 9/11 attacks, a compelling television special about New York firefighters was broadcast. The filmmakers had been working on a routine documentary showing what life inside a fire house was like. September 11 dawned as just another beautiful fall day. I was haunted as I watched them begin their day, the male camaraderie and joshing inside the house, the devotion to duty overlaid with boredom, the morning coffee and bagels, the quotidian gestures and conversation. But watching it, we all knew what happened next, what was waiting for them. We knew the outcome. It gave weight to every facial expression, every gesture, every breath they took. We breathed with them. The unbearable heaviness of being. It was heartbreaking to watch them race to the towers, then see them gather in the lobby because we knew they were planning and groping and rescuing in what would be a tomb for so many of them. To hear the thud of falling bodies. To see my friend, Catholic Chaplain Mychal Judge, his face a knot of concern. Then blackness. Then we saw his broken body gently and reverently laid on the altar of old St. Peter's, and as we watched we knew how many more would be borne up from the rubble. We witnessed the drama, knowing the end of the story.

> The resurrection of Jesus from the dead is the ground zero of human history and cosmic existence.

Søren Kierkegaard said "Purity of heart is to will one thing." For all of the many intellectual, cultural and theological eddies and streams that flow out of the great river of the Church, one strong, inexorable current feeds them all. The resurrection of Jesus from the dead is the ground zero of human history and cosmic existence.

My cousin, Walter Bouman, a teacher of the Church for many years at Trinity Seminary in Columbus, Ohio, recently died. He knew, we all know, the ending. And it gives added weight to every moment we live. In a sermon he preached at General Seminary in 1986, Walt said: "To be called to the mission of the reign of God is like reading the last chapter of a mystery novel without knowing the plot. That is, in fact, the way I read mysteries. I read enough at the beginning to find out who is murdered, who the main characters are. Then I skip to the last chapter to find out who did it. And that changes the way I read the novel."

Like watching doomed fire fighters living out their lives in the shadow of Ground Zero, we Christians live out of our understanding of the paschal mystery. We know how it all turned out, how it will all turn out. This knowledge of Calvary and the empty tomb gives a weight, a portent to our everyday lives and ministry as well. We attend to tragedy in our sadness to be sure, but we have read the last chapter, we know the end of the story. The ground zero of the resurrection of Jesus from the dead looms over every our every thought, song, gesture, ministry, and disaster response. It adds weight to our actions in the face of every tragedy, to every moment on our own homeward way. I said at Walt's funeral, "Knowing the end of the story means that we are laying to rest a conqueror today."

Blinded by the Light

> Let us not mock God with metaphor,
> analogy, sidestepping transcendence;
> Making of the event a parable, a sign painted in the
> faded credulity of earlier ages;
> Let us walk through the door.
>
> John Updike, Seven Stanzas at Easter

St. Paul was stunned by the resurrection of Jesus and never got over it. Paul experienced the resurrection of Jesus as both conversion and commissioning for ministry. I have been reflecting recently on Caravaggio's painting of the scene of the road to Damascus. Paul is flat on his back, legs splayed, arms lifted to heaven as he falls, his eyes shut, blinded by the resurrection light. The central figure in the painting is the horse, sensitively lifting its hoof to avoid treading on the poor creature sprawled beneath its belly in the dust. The encounter with the Risen Lord is a devastating encounter that lays Paul to the ground in absolute vulnerability. Paul knew and taught that to follow Jesus, to live the baptismal adventure, is to be utterly dependent on grace, always ready to be broken again by encounter with the truth, unprotected and needful. We are the blind man on the A Train of life, dependent on the presence of the Risen Lord active in the world, not seeing our destination but knowing the end of the story, hurtling through the tunnel toward the Day Approaching.

If Jesus beckons us beyond death, the future is open and hope and promise are possible. This is how I interpret the Reformation: as a pastoral call to get the end of the story right, to be vulnerable to the future beyond death, to give up death-denying justifications, to be placed by baptism into the death and resurrection of Jesus.

The resurrection of Jesus animates the way we read and interpret the Bible. Scripture is indispensable for the Church because it gives us the narratives of Israel, the cross and resurrection of Jesus, the birth of the Church. "Didn't our hearts burn within us...?" Is it any wonder, then, that in tragedy Nina's question is given the narrative of hope: Our lives have been re-enchanted by the resurrection of Jesus from the dead.

The Community of the Resurrection

God's most gracious response to the tragedy of human history is the Church, the community of the resurrection. But it is public Church, living its life in full view for the life of the world. *The Church is the Public Mission Table.* On the ground, that is our local congregation. Think of your home congregation, or of the one you remember from a former time in your life. People attend churches for many reasons. But at the end of the day, why do they persist in bringing themselves and their babies to the baptismal font? Why do they keep showing up? At the heart of the matter is Nina's question. The Church must speak its own truth, in season and out. The only ultimate security will never be found in this world. We will all die. We bring our children and ourselves to the baptismal font because at the end of the day it is here that Nina's question is answered. We place ourselves and our loved ones into the only secure place in this universe, into the arms of Jesus, who has promised that through his death and resurrection not even death can separate us from the love of God. The congregation exists to answer Nina's question in its life in the world.

What We Do
Our family had just returned home from a family vacation in Maine, having driven most of the day. It was evening. The phone rang as we entered our home. It was Dorothy, our dear friend. Her beloved husband Carmine had collapsed, she said, in the middle of their fiftieth wedding anniversary celebration. "We are at the emergency room at Holy Name. Please come." Dorothy and Carmine were like family to us, members of the congregation. As I was leaving, putting on a black shirt and collar over blue jeans, our son, Tim, maybe twelve at the time, said, "I'll go with you, Dad."

In the waiting room were the many friends and relatives, still dressed gaily in the tuxedos and gowns of the anniversary party. I pushed through doors that said, "Keep out." Carmine had just been pronounced dead. I went back out into the lobby. Everyone looked at me with Nina's question on their hearts. When there are no words, then we say the words of the Church. The life of a congregation's ministry goes out to the daily ground zeros of people's lives—to emergency rooms, hospital bedsides, places of death and hope and suffering—with the words of the Church that I shared in the emergency room after telling everyone that Carmine had died. "In my father's house are many rooms...." "I am the resurrection and the life...." "Yea, though I walk through the valley of the shadow of death...." We prayed, I hugged Dorothy, and finally Tim and I left. I drove about one hundred yards, pulled over, and put my head on the steering wheel to cry. Then Tim said softly, "So, Dad, that's what you do."

So, this is what we have been doing as the Church in the midst of the joys and tragedies of human living. We have been answering Nina's question with the Good News of the Resurrection of Jesus from the dead. The quotidian life of a congregation is reanimated when tragedy strikes. We have been baptized for these moments. We teach, by our words and by our actions, the hope and meaning of the resurrection of Jesus from the dead. We do this through our liturgies, our holy communions; in creating space for lamentations and in participating as healers of the breach, by incarnating the story of Jesus' victory over death on the cross and the triumph of the empty tomb. That grace is, always, all around us.

POINTS FOR REFLECTION AND DISCUSSION

1. *How do we do this work together in a culture that is so enthralled with the individual?*

2. *How do we express Good News beyond storytelling and listening? What might be the marks of a Church that takes seriously the task of Resurrection?*

3. *How do we reanimate in the absence of tragedy? How can the Church find ways to reanimate in the celebrations of life as well as amidst public tragedies?*

ACKNOWLEDGMENTS

To Stacy Martin and Ryan Cumming, who read the drafts and helped give shape to the book.

To my editor, Michael Coyne, who wrestled the book to the ground, knowing what material needed to be tossed out, and what needed to remain. I am grateful for what emerged from Michael's refiner's fire.

ABOUT THE AUTHOR

Stephen Bouman was the Bishop of the Metropolitan New York Synod of the Evangelical Lutheran Church in America on the day of the 9/11 attacks. He is a pastor, lecturer, author, and currently directs the domestic ministries of the ELCA. In his public ministry engaging issues which shape our communities—like disaster, race, peace, interfaith collaboration and immigration—he has depended on and pointed to the grace that pervades all around us.

Other Books from In Extenso Press

ALL THINGS TO ALL PEOPLE: A Catholic Church for the Twenty-First Century, by Louis DeThomasis, FSC, 118 pages, paperback

CATHOLIC BOY BLUES: A Poet's Journey of Healing, by Norbert Krapf, 224 pages, paperback

CATHOLIC WATERSHED: The Chicago Ordination Class of 1969 and How They Helped Change the Church, by Michael P. Cahill, 394 pages, paperback

CHRISTIAN CONTEMPLATIVE LIVING
Six Connecting Points, by Thomas M. Santa, CSSR, 126 pages, paperback

GREAT MEN OF THE BIBLE: A Guide for Guys
by Martin Pable, OFM Cap, 216 pages, paperback

THE GROUND OF LOVE AND TRUTH: Reflections on Thomas Merton's Relationship with the Woman Known as "M," by Suzanne Zuercher, OSB, 120 pages, paperback

HOPE: One Man's Journey of Discovery from Tormented Child to Social Worker to Spiritual Director, by Marshall Jung, 172 pages, paperback

MASTER OF CEREMONIES: A Novel
by Donald Cozzens, 288 pages, paperback and hardcover

NAVIGATING ALZHEIMER'S: 12 Truths about Caring for Your Loved One, by Mary K. Doyle, 112 pages, paperback

SHRINKING THE MONSTER: Healing the Wounds of Our Abuse, by Norbert Krapf, 234 pages, paperback

THE SILENT SCHISM: Healing the Serious Split in the Catholic Church by Louis DeThomasis, FSC, and Cynthia A. Nienhaus, CSA, 128 pages, paperback

THE UNPUBLISHED POET: On Not Giving Up on Your Dream
by Marjorie L. Skelly, 160 pages, paperback

WAYWARD TRACKS: Revelations about fatherhood, faith, fighting with your spouse, surviving Girl Scout camp... by Mark Collins, 104 pages, paperback

WE THE (LITTLE) PEOPLE, artwork by ISz, 50 plates, paperback

YOUR SECOND TO LAST CHAPTER: Creating a Meaningful Life on Your Own Terms, by Paul Wilkes, 120 pages, paperback and hardcover

AVAILABLE FROM BOOKSELLERS
OR FROM 800-397-2282 • INEXTENSOPRESS.COM
DISTRIBUTED EXCLUSIVELY BY ACTA PUBLICATIONS